AF182396

Beyond Rationality

An Imaginary Meeting between a Cat and a Psychoanalyst

Beyond Rationality

An Imaginary Meeting between a Cat and a Psychoanalyst

Vittorio Bizzozero

IFF BOOKS

London, UK
Washington, DC, USA

CollectiveInk

First published by iff Books, 2026
iff Books is an imprint of Collective Ink Ltd.,
Unit 11, Shepperton House, 89 Shepperton Road, London, N1 3DF
office@collectiveinkbooks.com
www.collectiveinkbooks.com
www.iff-books.com

For distributor details and how to order please visit the 'Ordering' section on our website.

Text copyright: Vittorio Bizzozero 2025

ISBN: 978 1 917991 07 0 (Paperback)
978 1 917991 25 4 (ebook)
Library of Congress Control Number: 2025942722

All rights reserved. Except for brief quotations in critical articles or reviews, no part of this book may be reproduced in any manner without prior written permission from the publishers.

The rights of Vittorio Bizzozero as author have been asserted in accordance with the Copyright, Designs and Patents Act 1988.

A CIP catalogue record for this book is available from the British Library.

Design: Lapiz Digital Services

UK: Printed and bound by CPI Group (UK) Ltd, Croydon, CR0 4YY
Printed in North America by CPI GPS partners

The manufacturer's authorised representative in the EU for product safety is:
eucomply OÜ - Pärnu mnt 139b-14, 11317 Tallinn, Estonia,
hello@ eucompliancepartner.com,
www.eucompliancepartner.com

What People Are Saying About

Beyond Rationality

Could we ever imagine — or even dream of — having a dialogue with a cat? This says much about the author's imaginative world. He becomes, in some way, a bit of a cat himself and takes us on a delightful journey between reality and fantasy.
Jacqueline Girard-Frésard, training analyst, Swiss Psychoanalytic Society; writer

Beyond Rationality is a thoughtful, delightful book that shows you the connection between wellness and being in nature. It is a delightful take on connecting with your surroundings not only by what you see, but what you feel.
Barbara Terrell, PMP, Cortez, Colorado, USA

Contents

Nature loves to hide. To know it, one must
listen with more than the mind.
— after Heraclitus

The way up and the way down are one and the same.
— Heraclitus

Preface

This book was born from a double movement: an encounter and a questioning.

The encounter was with a being who lives entirely in the present, outside the categories through which we humans attempt to tame the world — my cat. Day after day, in her silent, immediate presence, I began to glimpse another way of knowing: one that does not separate body and mind, sensation and thought, life and world.

The questioning was that of a psychoanalyst and a neuroscientist who, despite decades of study, continues to be astonished by the limits of what can be measured, codified, or explained. What is consciousness? Where does thought arise? Is the world ultimately countable, or does it exceed all measure?

The voice that carries these pages is both mine and not mine. In choosing to let my cat speak, I did not seek to anthropomorphize her, nor to project human theories into an animal mind. Rather, I wished to loosen the grip of our rational categories, to allow another form of intuition to emerge — one that belongs to the living fabric of nature itself.

You will not find in this book a linear argument, a system, or a doctrine. It is a dialogue, a meditation, a poetic and philosophical wandering. A reflection on time, space, life, death, and the mystery that binds them all.

Science remains essential, and psychoanalysis offers invaluable tools. But beyond rationality, there is the breath of the world, the rhythm of nature, the silent pulse of the One. To sense it, we must sometimes step aside — or perhaps, simply listen.

This book is an invitation to such listening.

It is dedicated to those who remain curious — and to those who know that curiosity is inseparable from wonder.

Vittorio Bizzozero
Geneva, 2025

Introduction

This book is the result of a curious and improbable meeting — between a man (a psychoanalyst trained in neuroscience) and an imaginary cat. What unfolds is a dialogue between two ways of knowing: one rational and analytical, grounded in science and reason; the other intuitive, poetic, and instinctive, grounded in experience.

This is not a debate between science and imagination. It's a meeting — sometimes serious, sometimes playful — between different forms of intelligence. The one that dominates today's world values calculation, prediction, and logic. But there is another kind: one that senses rather than proves, that listens rather than explains.

What happens when we let go of the idea that only what can be measured is real? What if we trust not only what we see, but what we feel — what we imagine, dream, or remember? This book invites you into that space.

Its structure follows the rhythm of a psychoanalytic session: associative, wandering, often nonlinear. You may find echoes more than arguments, resonances rather than conclusions. It is meant to be read not with the goal of understanding everything, but with a sense of openness — letting some parts speak directly to your intuition.

The cat speaks in the first person. Her words may seem surreal at times, or poetic, or strange. That's fine. She is not here to deliver facts, but to open doors.

Perhaps this journey will feel familiar. Or perhaps it will feel like stepping into another kind of consciousness altogether — one that sees time as circular, space as alive, and presence as a form of knowing.

Welcome to a dialogue that goes beyond rationality.

Chapter 1

Not Everything Is Measurable

I am more attuned to the rhythms of poetry than to units of distance. Measurement, though useful, threatens to flatten our uniqueness as living beings. The metric system can help us describe the world, but it also risks silencing the subtle signs that emerge within it.

And what are those signs? Can we truly feel them, interpret them, trust them? Or are we always in danger of speaking over them – replacing nature's whisper with the echo of our own voice?

My writer and I are preoccupied with this dilemma – it lies at the very heart of how we communicate. How does he tune into my thoughts and transform them into language? Can he really sense what I experience? Or is he simply drawing a feline outline of himself?

Perhaps he is giving shape to something that exists only in potential – an idea that never fully becomes a form. We don't know, and maybe we don't need to. It happens. He writes what he thinks I'm thinking. Without him, this book wouldn't exist. Without me, it would have no reason to exist. We write together. We co-create. And no matter where our ideas come from, they appear – and neither of us claims exclusivity over them.

Perhaps it's the same with nature. Whether or not it speaks to us – or whether we simply assign it meaning – the essential thing is that we think together, not as spectators, but as participants. We're not standing outside nature, studying it from a distance. We are part of the same phenomenon, involved in the very act of observing.

Scientific research is invaluable, of course. But not all research is the same. Some paths rely on statistics. Others emerge from intuition. Still others are spun from abstract mathematics. What matters is that we remain open to each form of knowing — and to the limits of each.

And yet my writer quickly returns to what he knows. This shows that we don't always do what we say — or write. Here lies our first difficulty, since he tends to take the lead. This impulse — to frame, define, control — reveals itself everywhere, not just in science but also in daily life. We rush to interpret, often before we've truly seen.

Right now, as he types on his tablet, I rest my cheek on the hand holding it. He writes with the other. Sometimes I extend a paw, placing it on the edge of the screen. He finds this charming, as if I want to be part of the writing process. And maybe I do. But when my paw touches the screen, the cursor freezes. He gently moves it aside, careful not to catch a stray claw. A romantic observer might say I'm leaving my mark. A pragmatic one might see only a sleepy cat resting beside a human.

Another observer would see my head tenderly resting on his hand, notice my half-closed eyes — a state of relaxation and well-being. A researcher might count the number of interactions in our exchanges. But not everything is observable, since no one will be able to see what I feel. And even I don't always know what I'm experiencing.

Ah! I forgot to tell you — I'm a girl.

Chapter 2

Seeing and Being Seen

Let me return to what I feel in this moment — my head resting tenderly on the hand that holds the tablet. There is a deep calm here, the opposite of anxiety. I'm utterly relaxed, safe. My half-closed eyes reflect the love I feel for him.

As I daydream, he types. Don't look for direct communication here. I imagine; he writes. He wanders through language; I drift through images. Is there a connection? We don't know. It simply happens.

I often imagine the minds of people as glowing points just above their foreheads. Each weekend, when my writer arrives at the mill — where I live all week — I sit at the small table near the entrance. He leans down, I tilt my head, and he kisses me gently right between the eyes. Our minds meet.

Perhaps I'm sensitive to people's inner states. Perhaps we are communicating — mind to mind — without words. But must everything be explained? Must every phenomenon be accounted for?

If everything could be explained, the world might become lifeless — overrun by rational thought, with creativity shackled and caged. What a bleak image!

I see the world directly. My consciousness is primary. As Gerald Edelman, the neurobiologist, once said: animals live in the present. We exist without the burden of past or future. Our awareness isn't mediated by representation. We see; we sense; we respond.

Lately, something has changed in me. I've grown curious about what's behind things — inside closets, behind curtains. My writer noticed this, along with my weight gain, and assumed I was preparing to give birth. But what he interpreted as a hormonal shift is actually a perceptual one. Like the glowing point I imagine above his head, I'm drawn to what is hidden, to the unseen parts of my world.

Chapter 3

Dreaming in Dimensions

Last night, my writer had a dream. He was facing a geometric challenge. He saw a shimmering solid — a dodecahedron — with 12 sharply defined pentagonal faces. Hovering around it was another structure, almost invisible and vibrating, made of countless facets. It enveloped the dodecahedron like a breathing skin.

This second shape had an infinite number of facets and was driven by a kind of vibration that made it blurry, in contrast to the solid it concealed, which was clearly outlined. It was as if the envelope emphasized the dodecahedron, which struck the eye with its pronounced relief and the brilliance of its faces.

It seems to me that he's having increasingly complex dreams. I try to discover new corners of the house, while he throws himself into improbable geometries. He argues that, in a book written by Anthelme Éduard Chaignet, the author explains that in Pythagorean thought, the four elements — earth, fire, air, and water — are likened to figures, or rather, are actual solid figures, also called "mathematics." The sphere contains the cube, from which comes earth; from the pyramid or tetrahedron comes fire; from the octahedron comes air; from the icosahedron comes water; and the dodecahedron constitutes the sphere of the Whole. This fifth element, this quintessence, is ether — where the luminous stars live and feed, seemingly motionless and fixed to the vault of the sky.

Apparently, our points of view are at odds: I explore what lies behind the red curtain; he soars toward antiquity and the vault of the sky. There is, however, a certain resemblance between his dream and my vision of the little dot. Could our two visions overlap — mine addressing the minds of people, his taking him to the higher spheres of nature? Perhaps this shows how we function: each of us explores an extreme. I am in the world; he tries to find an abstract representation of it.

Perhaps, by flying into abstract geometries, he draws closer to my inner world. And I, in turn, must stay grounded so he doesn't drift too far from this one.

We balance each other. He ascends; I anchor. He dreams; I watch. Without him, my thoughts wouldn't find words. Without me, his words might lose their grounding.

The Texture of Space

When I move through a room, I don't see open space. I see a series of known points — places tied to memory, to scent, to feeling. For me, space isn't continuous; it's made of familiar islands, each one alive with meaning.

For example, I never enter the house through the main door, which is near the path that separates the house from the pond and the surrounding land. It's along this small, little-used path that my writer arrives with his car. I avoid the main entrance and prefer to use the French window that opens directly into the living room. For me, the choice of door changes the layout of the house, and if I take the other door, I feel a little lost.

When I venture into the house, I follow certain routes that are always the same, as if the space were made up of lines without me being able to reach the surface. In this space there are of course central points like the armchair in which my friend sits to read or write, his wooden bed from another century, and the place next to the sink where I can get milk. I have the impression that I know the outside of the house better, perhaps because the wide space suits me better and especially because I walk through it a lot at night. I don't have an overall view of the place. I have more of a detailed view than a panoramic view. I point my senses at objects with my eyes, my ears, and my nose. When I am very close I also use my cheeks, some say to mark my territory, but I also do it to try to get to know him better; that's what I often do when I am on my friend's lap. Do I have a notion of time? Usually I follow my own rhythm. However, when I stay inside for the night, I lie down next to my writer's head; I sleep sometimes and watch over him at others. During the day, it's the opposite: he watches over me when I sleep on his lap, and sometimes he sleeps too if he's napping in his chair. I go to bed at night when he goes to sleep, and he gets up early in the morning to let me out. So we're pretty well in sync.

Human beings see rooms, walls, and open areas. They map them, measure them. But for me, space is alive. It quivers. It holds traces of movement, scent, and sound. Nothing is fixed. Everything is breathing.

My awareness is close-range. My world comes into focus when I am near — near to a chair leg, a shoe, the crack beneath a door. I don't scan the horizon; I dive into textures. I explore edges, borders, corners. I listen with my paws, my whiskers, my tail.

Your eye allows you to have an overview of your surroundings, and when you focus on an object, you don't lose sight of the whole; moreover, you can calibrate the distance between objects and take into account the proximity relationships between them. I can't do all that. My eye looks for details more than the whole; it can point at a specific object as if it were out of context. As I often say, I can only do one thing at a time. I cannot look at two objects at the same time and it is impossible for me to decide if there is a relationship between them. On the other hand, I am sensitive to the texture of space and I do not see space as something contiguous. I perceive space as if it were formed of small grains that reveal voids and interstices. To put it more simply, it is as if I see a set of small points that concentrate to form a figure when I fix my gaze; otherwise it is as if there are holes. It is as if these small points come together to form an object when I look, and otherwise, when I am not pointing at an object, they appear like a moving and vibrant cloud. My writer explained to me that when he writes on his tablet something similar happens: first of all the word that appears on the screen is not continuous — it is made up of infinite points that come together to form the figures of writing; moreover, the word that appears stable on the screen is the result of an oscillation that makes the screen turn off and on a hundred times per second. This gives you an idea of how I perceive the world, which does not appear as compact to me as it does to you. This is why any change in my environment sometimes provokes my curiosity and often panic, as if I can no longer find my usual bearings, but above all as if all the small points that make up my space are going in all directions, like a disordered cloud.

It's like when you shake a wasps' nest — it creates confusion and they go in all directions, before probably attacking you. For me something similar happens: the change of position of an object, of the arrangement of the furniture, sometimes even the arrival of a new person, produces chaos in me, and I have the impression that I no longer control my little points or even that they could turn against me. This happens to me especially inside the inhabited part of the house, never outside. Why this difference between the two places? When I am in nature, in the small forest behind the house, by the pond on the other side of the path, or in the fields that stretch as far as the eye can see in front of and behind the house, I never have this unpleasant impression of disorder. Of course, nature changes, but it does so very slowly, imperceptibly, like my hair which grows in winter and which reduces when the weather turns warm. Humans talk about a comfort zone, of course when they talk about their homes, but also when they stick to their habits of thought. My comfort zone is nature. Inside the house I also have comfort zones; the armchair in which my writer reads and writes is my focal point — it's where I spend a lot of time on his lap, and where I sleep, smooth my fur, or simply relax with my eyes half-open. There's also his old bed on which I spend my nights when my writer is there. As for the rest of the house, I only pass through it, as if this space were unknown to me or frightened me. My writer thinks that I live like humans before they built homes, even before they took refuge in caves. I think that when they found themselves inside for the first time they were perhaps frightened of no longer having direct contact with the ground, of no longer seeing the vegetation and especially the sky. Apparently, humans who live in cities sometimes have plants they call "indoor." At our mill, all the plants are outside. Apparently, there are also indoor cats that never go outside, or if they do, they end up in the street with cars. I've never met any of these cats, and when the mill's former owners wanted to move to the city, I immediately left to go back to the mill, 20 kilometers away. I don't like being cooped up, and I don't think I can stand being inside for longer than a certain amount of time.

An idea came to me. What if, by losing direct and permanent contact with nature, by shutting themselves away in enclosed spaces, humans had then focused on what they call their "internal world" and started to believe that everything revolved around them? When I'm in nature, I merge with it, I am with it, I am part of it. Inside the house I lose contact with this feeling of being one with it — it's as if all my senses were turning against me and I was creating a kind of laboratory nature. I then have visions; I have the impression that space becomes punctiform since it is no longer in balance between sky and earth, my true coordinates; I see shadows; I am afraid of black mirrors — they are the radiators that heat the house in winter — and of the chaos caused by any change. My writer thinks that I am fleeing to the outside, when I am only running toward what is for me the true existence. When I am with my writer, I sometimes forget my love for nature. It allows me to experience different emotions and I discover a new pleasure, that of being loved.

Chapter 4

Dreaming and Sleeping

My writer had a dream last night. He was with a woman. There was a strong attraction that drew them together. They kissed on the mouth, and then part of my writer's body — one of his hands — detached itself from him and found itself in the woman's hands, while still feeling the same sensations, as if his hand were still part of his body. He thought that even though we are separated by geographical distance, it's as if we are part of the same body and can communicate remotely, instantly, without crossing the space that separates us, without any connection or transmission.

Moreover, the writing hand is not entirely his; it is the instrument that unites our thoughts. It's Friday, and tomorrow he'll be heading to the mill. We might understand this dream in the following way: during sleep, a part of us detaches from ourselves to live experiences that are hidden from us when we are awake.

Besides, why do we say "myself" or "ourselves," if not to convince ourselves that in sleep and in the waking state we remain the same? That's not certain — just as it's not certain that two people nearby are the same as when they're separated by distance. But here, my friend has once again wandered into improbable conjectures. I've noticed that he tends to overcomplicate our thinking when trying to explain a phenomenon.

Let's be simpler! Let's just admit that we live in two worlds that are both opposed and superimposed — like day and night, like light and dark. Even during the day, my life is divided between presence and absence, between the interior of the house and the nature that awaits me outside — even if talking about "inside" and "outside" makes no sense to my cat's mind.

I'm tired now, and I can no longer follow what my writer is trying to demonstrate. He needs me to help him out of his dead end. I go to sleep, where the sun warms the ground of the terrace.

And now I'm dreaming in my turn: I am standing on a stake, surrounded by intense colors. They are the large leaves of a tree that hide part of my body. Only my head emerges from the foliage, and I look far away, my eyes fixed on the horizon. I wonder, in the dream, if the stake is part of a fence or if it stands alone in the middle of the fields. I can't make it out clearly, but it seems to me that this stake is connected to others by barbed wire — though I cannot see them, since I'm looking straight ahead.

What struck me were not shapes but colors — intense colors. It was my writer who gave them names: sun yellow and Mars red. But in my dream, the yellow was truly that of the sun — a bright yellow — while the red was blood red. My writer told me he saw similar reds in the sunsets he once observed in Patagonia, in the far south of the southern hemisphere.

Descriptions or explanations don't matter — it's my friend's habit to always want to describe sensory impressions. I return to my impressions, since descriptions aren't my specialty. Two colors, then: one, the yellow of the sun at its highest; the other, the red after it has set on the horizon. Two splendid colors shared the foliage of my tree.

And as Heraclitus, one of the philosophers of antiquity — and one of my friend's favorites — said: "How can anyone hide from that which never sets?" Here's what he says about our question regarding waking and sleeping:

> As in the nighttime a man kindles for himself a light,
> so when a living man lies down in death with his vision extinguished,
> he attaches himself to the state of death;

even as one who has been awake lies down with his vision
extinguished
and attaches himself to the state of sleep.

Everyone will understand this in their own way, but it speaks to me about my dream. Could the yellow and red be like lights that appear during the night of my sleep? I look toward the horizon. From within sleep, could I be looking toward the horizon of waking life? The barbed wire of the fence I'm in might mean it's forbidden to pass from sleep to waking without injuring oneself on brambles.

We might also think of the river of forgetfulness – Lethe – whose water had to be drunk when returning from the realm of the dead to the world of the living. But then, in our sleep, are we both lit and extinguished at the same time?

Chapter 5

Remote Attachment

My writer took a short nap and woke up feeling as if I were resting on his arm. At first, when I hadn't yet gotten used to his presence, he found a way to get me to come home: he'd take a short nap, and just as he was falling asleep, I'd run up to him. That's what just happened — he fell asleep and immediately felt my presence on the arm he uses to write. I'm at his side so he can resume our writing.

In fact, before taking his nap, lacking inspiration, he sent two of the photos he'd taken of me last weekend to one of his printers. One of them shows me resting my cheek against the hand holding his tablet, with one paw on its edge. Clearly, when I thought I was connected remotely, he didn't quite believe it. Now he feels my presence directly, even though he's in the city and I'm at the mill.

For him, it seems incredible because he's still caught up in rational reasoning. For me, it's self-evident. Our love binds us, regardless of any kind of thought transmission or other connection that might cross the space separating us. It's like what they call "nonlocality" in quantum physics, but for us, it happens in the immediate present, and we don't have the means to study a pair of photons entangled across light-years.

Besides, any attempt to link what my writer and I are experiencing with quantum theory would be frowned upon by the scientific community. I believe what we're living has nothing to do with particle physics, and referring to it only distracts us from our subject. It would be borrowing a theory from one field to avoid thinking deeply about our own reality at a distance.

So, let's get back to work. I think it's impossible to explain — or even understand — why I would manifest just as my writer is falling asleep. Whether the distance between us is a hundred meters or a hundred kilometers makes no difference.

We've reflected on sleep and wondered whether the world of sleep holds surprises for us. Of course, there are dreams, and most people believe that during part of sleep, they live inside those dreams. But what if dreams are only images we create as we return from sleep to wakefulness?

How often has my writer heard people say, "I never dream" or "I never remember my dreams"? Perhaps for them, the transition between sleep and wakefulness is abrupt. He once told me about a patient who was seized with panic when waking up — as if she could no longer return to her usual reality.

We say someone "falls asleep," and sometimes people, as they drift off, feel as if they're falling and suddenly wake up with a start. But I'd like to reflect on this phrase attributed to Heraclitus: "In his sleep and with his eyes extinguished, he burns more than the dead." And also: "Man is lit and extinguished like a light during the night."

These sayings are enigmatic. There's a reason Heraclitus was called "the obscure," even in antiquity. One could interpret this to mean that sleep is both light — we access another reality — and darkness — because that reality extinguishes when we wake. But why would a sleeper "burn more than the dead"?

Perhaps in our sleep we burn — what we perceive scorches our senses — but we are also close to death, both burning and extinguished. And maybe, through sleep, we open a door beyond which space is no longer passable and time becomes mere simultaneity.

But for now, I'm the one making the journey into my writer's sleep. If he does the same, it's still happening without his awareness.

Take my writer, for example — just seconds after falling asleep, he wakes with a start, sensing I've landed on his right arm. He felt the physical weight of me and also visualized my presence just before opening his eyes.

Of course, one could say this is simply autosuggestion — he wants to prove we can communicate at a distance. And that's fair. But we believe that reason is sometimes wrong — or rather, that it can only grasp a certain kind of reality.

Think about it: Does everything you feel have a reason? Does everything that passes through your mind have an explanation? Is everything observable?

Physicists have speculated about a probabilistic world, the nonlocality of particles, 11 dimensions, and dark matter absorbing the energy of known particles. They estimate that three-quarters of our universe is made up of things we don't understand.

So, can I believe that while my writer sleeps, I appear beside him, even if we're separated by 150,000 meters? Yes, we experience this every day in our writing — whether I'm on his lap, sleeping, or he's in another country, or even flying over an ocean.

Perhaps this connection happens when one of us sleeps, or when we both sleep — or even when we're both awake. Maybe the part of us that sleeps at night also dozes within us when we're awake. We say our head is "in the clouds," our mind "elsewhere," our thoughts "in the west." Are we still really here?

Have you ever wondered why children fear ghosts in wardrobes or monsters under their beds or behind the curtains? Sure, these are common fears — phobias even — and phobias can be explained.

But what if children have easier access to the world of sleep than you? What if they can cross the river of forgetfulness and gaze into Tartarus?

In mythology, Ouranos — the sky — stretched above the earth and was governed by day and night. Beneath the earth lay Tartarus, ruled by Erebus, the darkness of the Underworld. Tartarus was the opposite of the sky — a kind of mirror reflection beneath the surface.

Let's return to Heraclitus: "If you don't expect the unexpected, you won't find it, because it is hard to find and difficult." And again, on sleep: "All things we see while awake are death — Thanatos — just as all things we see while asleep are sleep."

Meow! This is all getting a bit too complicated for me. Maybe it frightens you too — it's like a world turned upside down... not a vision of life, but of stillness, something close to death. A frozen view of the world.

There may be more life in sleep, where life only seems to be sleeping. We cats are lucky — we sleep most of the time. We doze, but we are not dead.

My writer once attended a scientific talk where the speaker mentioned Schrödinger's cat and said it saddened him to imagine the cat being both dead and alive. He preferred to think of the cat as both asleep and awake. I liked that. It highlights my specialty — sleep.

About what lies dormant in us: my writer told me that Sigmund Freud founded psychoanalysis with a great book about the interpretation of dreams, published at the turn of the twentieth century. In that cornerstone work, he introduced the term *unbewusst*, translated into English as "unconscious."

But *unbewusst* also means "involuntary," "instinctive," "unaware," "senseless," and even "irrational" or "mad." A rich word. And by translating it with a single term, much of that richness was lost.

Now imagine how we could connect all those meanings to what has been said about sleep.

Before inventing psychoanalysis, Freud used hypnosis — suggesting thoughts or emotions that could help patients feel better. That, too, was a journey through sleep. Even the psychoanalytic couch, where patients lie down and freely associate, is meant to bring them closer to the sleeping state — bypassing logic and reason.

Let's return to that foundational book, which talks more about dreams than sleep. Understandably so: how can one describe sleep when, in sleep, we lose consciousness?

I don't believe that applies to me. That's why I can tell my writer what I feel when I sleep. Without me, this book we're writing wouldn't make sense. My friend might still think that the unconscious only shows itself in dreams, and that dreams merely guard sleep.

But why would I spend three-quarters of my life sleeping?

Interestingly, physicists say that dark matter also occupies three-quarters of the universe. Maybe it's time we think more about sleep — about darkness — rather than always chasing the light. Otherwise, we risk missing most of what exists.

Call upon poets, sci-fi writers, musicians — all those who use a different metric than the meter. Ask small children, lovers of fantasy, even the mad. Freud began with hysterical women. His teacher Charcot once said they defied the laws of anatomy. They had convulsions, paralysis, spasms, and suffocation — without any detectable organic cause.

It was a first shock to conventional medicine, which, even a century later, often considers unexplained symptoms to be, let's say, "in people's heads." Just joking! What I mean is: anything that doesn't fit doctors' protocols is labeled as psychological. We laugh about that a lot.

That's why my writer and I have replaced the word "psyche" with "state of mind." Yes — sleep may not be visible, and perhaps it should be measured with the mind, not just with electrodes.

That's why we cats are here. Our dreams aren't like yours. We have visions. Our visions are more fixed, while your dreams unfold into stories. We think your dreams reflect your past and present state of mind — and also depict how you're returning to wakefulness… from sleep.

Let me tell you about my last vision.

I was in a forest, surrounded by tall grass that blocked my view. In front of me, only green. But I heard deep voices from the forest — a monotonous vibration. The birds had gone quiet. The leaves stood still; the wind no longer played with them. And again, that deep, almost mechanical vibration.

In the distance, I could hear the faint cries of birds, as if they wanted to flee the too-silent place.

Could I be in contact with the world of sleep?

What if the world of sleep doesn't exist at all — but is a product of our imagination, like Alice's world, beyond the mirror of what we believe we perceive — of what we believe is real?

What if reality is just an illusion created by our senses?

Then we would be caught between two illusions: one of the day, and one of the night.

But what happens, then, when my writer feels my full weight on his arm and sees me — just before opening his eyes?

Mystery.

We don't want to prove anything — just to share our experience.

And our experience offers a sign. It shows that we can communicate without language, regardless of distance. Like from one small point to another. Like a point at the intersection of two lines. A point where waking and sleeping meet. A point on a scale with no measure.

Chapter 6

Observation and/or Intuition

Phew! I feel exhausted after that discussion. I'm going to stop thinking about all this and tell you about my daily life with my writer. Today, he understood one of the functions of my tail. He was next to me, and with the tip of it, I tapped his hand and then wrapped it around his wrist. He was amazed to see this new way of speaking to him, a new way of showing him that I'm in contact with him and that I appreciate his presence and friendship, a way of letting him know that I love him and am attached to him, tapping and squeezing his wrist, a way of experiencing a hug and kissing him once more. For me, this was also a discovery, since I usually wag my tail in different ways, from left to right in an energetic movement or more calmly and regularly, and also many other scenarios that I won't go into detail about. But this way of tapping the back of his hand and wrapping the tip of my tail around his wrist was a discovery, even for me. It just goes to show that not everything has been catalogued by those who claim to know everything about our feline behavior. It was a new game for me, a way to communicate without resorting to sleep. I want to open a new discussion here. This certainly concerns cats, but also humans. Let's start with us cats. Why do humans study our behavior and decide that this means that? How many times have we heard it said: he rubs against his owner's legs to mark his territory, to deposit his pheromones... Since when does behavior have to be coded unequivocally? The problem with this type of assertion is that these people want to confine us to a single explanation. But what's more serious is limiting our lives to a pure observation of some of our outward manifestations. Don't we have the right to an inner life, to emotions, feelings, thoughts? Once again, what is foregrounded is observation; what is not visible does not exist. And here, my writer and I are taking on the battle against those who are obsessed with behavior, against those who think the eye decides what we should think, against those who confuse seeing with being, against all sorts of Saint Thomases — Thomas the Apostle, symbol of disbelief and distrust. Wow, this little crusade against the extreme observationists has done us good. Far be it from us to criticize all the observers who have enlightened our civilization since antiquity. What we want to emphasize is that there is also a science without measurement. For example, when Pythagoras asserted that the Earth is round, he did so based on an intuition: since a sphere is the perfect shape, the universe in general could only be spherical. So let's allow observation and intuition to coexist. Moreover, one of these predecessors, Anaximander, loved to measure; he reportedly wrote a treatise on geometry, calculated the height of the sun, and tried to construct a sphere representing the Earth. But let's not be mistaken! All great discoveries have succeeded in combining measurement, calculation, and intuition. The difficulty perhaps lies in the requirement that science has to demonstrate or prove its intuitions. Obviously, in the minds of many scientists there are all sorts of intuitions awaiting demonstrations. Why not share their intuitions with us before they are subjected to the test of measurements? Of course, intuition also comes into play after measurement.

For example, when physicists at CERN think that there could be dark photons that absorb the energy of known particles and when they think that dark matter would occupy three-quarters of our space, it is indeed an intuition, certainly based on measurements made, but perhaps also preceding their measurement. The transition from measurement to theory also implies a construction that calls for a certain intuition. Therefore, there is never a direct transition between experimentation and theorization, and nothing is ever definitively proven. On the other hand, when we confuse experiment and results, that is to say when we want to prove a phenomenon solely by its statistical significance, we risk relating anything we want. In statistics, a result is said to be statistically significant when it is improbable that it was obtained by simple chance. Therefore, it is possible to relate any phenomenon to any other. Without intuition, we would be in the presence of an improbable probabilism — I'll let you play with those two words. My writer likes to quote certain sentences out of context. "They make me hate things that seem likely when they are planted in me as infallible," said Michel de Montaigne in his *Essays*. I can't even read, and he offers me complicated sentences. Yet this idea touches me because everything I experience seems true to me, and I don't like truths that are never wrong. For example, for me, the fact of presenting myself while my writer is asleep is something that seems true to me, but I wouldn't make it an indubitable generalization. If I participate in this writing, it's also to show you that I don't see the world like you. I told you that my primary consciousness forbids me any reference to the past or any projection into the future. My perception is also primary since I see directly, as if I were one with the object; I cannot represent the world — the world presents itself to me without my being able to filter it mentally. This is certainly a disadvantage for me, yours being that if your filter is too thick your way of thinking about nature will prevent you from seeing it. We quote Heraclitus again: "What we see and take, we leave; what we neither see nor take, we take away." As always Heraclitus touches me, since I too take what I do not see; that is to say that for me perception does not consist only in seeing an object, in defining it with the help of my sensory organs, but perception also goes the other way — the object reaches me without me being able to actively perceive it. Is this too complicated? An example? What my writer explained to me about people who have lost their sense of smell and then suddenly regain it: they have the feeling that the world is entering them. Or, for me, when a change occurs in the house, I feel threatened, since my perception can no longer fixate on the object. But Heraclitus's statement also tells us that what we take in is not what we see.

All this detour is to tell you that not everything is observable and that perhaps we unwittingly take in what we don't see.

Chapter 7

The World Doesn't Revolve around Our Head

Let's continue on our path. Last night, my writer dreamed of a wedding. He only remembers the face of the bride facing him. She had a white ribbon around her forehead, as if her veil had been wrapped around her head. He may have been the groom, but he wasn't represented in the dream. He looked around him as if he were the groom, with his eyes. He could see that he was wearing a black suit. There may also have been a priest. All this was happening outside, at the end of a pergola that was like a corridor decorated with pink flowers. If I were his psychoanalyst, I could tell him that this is our wedding through our writing, and that he has his eyes fixed on me so that I can continue to inspire him and unveil the mysteries of nature – all its pink flowers that adorn the path of the pergola. I could also point out to him that our eyes only allow us to see outside ourselves, or at most a part of our body, and that we must rely on the eyes of others to see ourselves. This is where my writer visualizes another plot, that of Dante ascending to heaven by staring into the eyes of Beatrice, his inspiration. What would this association tell him? That it is time to elevate his thought above the observable? That the moment has come for him to approach the higher spheres of the mind? If we compare my writer's dream and the vision that presented itself to his mind, there are similarities. Of course, you will say, it was he who associated them, the vision did not fall from the sky, and you would be right. This does not prevent us from doing the exercise. In both there is a corridor, horizontal in the dream, vertical and ascending in the association. In both he fixes his eyes on the eyes of a woman. In one, the solution is on earth, in the other in heaven. We'll stop here and leave you, for now, to pursue your own associations. And as Heraclitus would have said: "The obscure neither expresses nor hides thought, but indicates it."

Our obscure philosopher again: "Most live as if they had an intelligence of their own." This opens another question that fascinates us: whether humans are ready to accomplish a revolution like Copernicus's, whether they are ready to renounce the idea that everything revolves around their heads. What's incredible is to learn that more than 25 centuries ago someone had already thought of this, and that despite the fact that several sciences have taken the step toward Copernicus, others, such as medicine and psychology, persist in viewing the world from our nervous structures or our internal world. Sigmund Freud had indeed attempted on several occasions to take the step outside the cranium, by reflecting on the importance of the quantities of excitations that modify our psychic quality, on the existence of a force that would push us toward the inanimate world, on the presence of a censorship that would prohibit us from certain thoughts. However, he isolated the individual in what he called "psychic reality." On the clinical level, all the cards were at his disposal to open the individual outside of himself; free association was to free the patient from rational thought; transference was to allow the patient to shift his internal world onto the analyst. Then there was the importance of the framework that could shape the patient's words, the involvement of the analyst who took his place as an analytical partner. There was also the idea that the thoughts that arise in analysis no longer belong to one or the other. Everything seems to be ready for psychoanalysis, paradoxically, to no longer revolve around the patient. It would become a dialogue like the one my writer and I have, where each inspires the other and this forces us to take paths that we had not initially imagined, neither of us taken separately. It is true that for us it is perhaps easier — this is paradoxical — to dialogue since my vision of the world is so different from his way of thinking. Thanks to this dialogue, each of us changes and it is not because I am a cat that I must necessarily continue to mark my territory and sharpen my claws to make myself interesting. And he does not need to lock himself in the world of logic, of causality, and especially in what is statistically proven by a victory against chance.

Chapter 8

Dionysus and the Dismemberment

Here I return to my daily life. My friend has put on some Native American music. These drums beat a heavy rhythm, with a flute trying to exist by sharpening its notes. And the drums become more and more oppressive... I got scared and went out onto the terrace, onto a stone that must have once been part of a fireplace. I took shelter from the rain and leaned against the wall of the house. I preferred being in touch with the sounds of nature rather than enduring this monotonous musical structure, with occasional guttural voices rising from the depths of the earth or women's cries trying to lift the vitality of the whole.

From my stone, I observed the movement in the small forest. Right in front of me, there was a squirrel searching for something in the wet grass. I stared at it intently; it didn't seem to notice me. I also saw that my friend was looking in the same direction — at the squirrel, who continued exploring the base of the trees, which he certainly knows better than we do. Now I'm meowing because I want to go back into the house. Once inside, I sit on his lap and press my paws alternately on his belly; this comforts me.

The music has changed: the drums have gone silent, and string instruments now accompany the flute, which seems softer. I feel more in harmony with this music — the percussion, especially the drums, unsettles me. Now I'm asleep. I wonder if he can travel in my sleep. I know that today he was wondering how I manage to spend hours in the same place without doing any research or activity.

Now I feel that he's found the point of contact — maybe it's this airy music... I feel weightless, as if I'm levitating above the world, as if I'm in direct contact with his thoughts. I see his thoughts taking shape, like little dots forming words. It's as if the words are coming from me, as if I'm truly experiencing what I think deep down. No — it's more than that. It's as if his words are transformed into impressions that reach me.

Now I rest my cheek against his hand, I purr, and I believe we are in sync. Now he can truly begin to write. I feel a deep peace; I believe there are no images, only a feeling of unity with everything. Images would tear me away from this sensation. I become one, without words... soon even the sensations will fade, and he won't be able to write anymore... it's silence...

He falls asleep, and we share this moment, just the two of us...

Waking from this shared silence, he thought to himself that I was the coolest cat in the world, and that meditation had probably been invented by cats like me. And it's true: with all the hours I spend sleeping, dozing, grooming, purring, and watching the nature around me, my active life amounts to only a short part of my existence. It's true that when he's around, my life revolves around him and his around mine — especially since we began sharing this writing.

I think he's learning from me how to look at the colors of the sky differently, and I'm learning from him how to wander through my visions. He's learning that representations aren't the only things that matter — that he can let his imagination roam freely — and I'm learning that even if I stay in the same place for long periods without moving, I still live, I still am. I opened his eyes to a world without measure, and he taught me that those who claim to be experts on cats often miss the mark, because they tend to reduce us to standard behaviors. But my writer and all those who love us know how to listen and be sensitive to our secret lives.

The Titans gave little Dionysus a mirror that allowed them to dismember the child and devour him. The young god was surprised by the Titans, who distracted him with toys, including the mirror. He tried to escape them, turning successively into a lion, a tiger, a horse, a snake, and a bull — but they killed him, dismembered him, and devoured the pieces of his corpse. Zeus ordered Apollo to gather and bury his limbs. As for the heart, which remained intact, Athena took it and gave it to Zeus. The Titans were cast into Tartarus, reduced to ashes, and from their ashes the human race was born — and in each human, there lives a piece of Dionysus's heart.

All this is to say that we too have been dismembered by people who've tried to dissect our behavior and given us a mirror in which we cannot recognize ourselves. Fortunately, a part of our heart remains alive in those humans who cherish our uniqueness.

Of course, we could interpret the myth of Dionysus in countless ways. For example, we might think that conventional medicine has also dismembered you into parts, and that every time you visit your doctor, you bring them one of your pieces. For us cats, it's a bit different, because our lives sometimes matter less than yours. But first, you'll have to choose whether you want to bring them a piece of your body or a piece of your mind. If you choose the latter, you'll be referred to a psychologist, a psychiatrist, or perhaps — but more rarely — a psychoanalyst. Even there, it can be complicated, since even there, you might be dismembered — sorry, diagnosed with multiple conditions. But here, you'll be heard, and your personality — and your whole being — will be taken into account.

On the other hand, if you made the first choice — that of the general practitioner — dismemberment may occur, and perhaps necessarily so, because your doctor was trained that way. If they change paradigms — their reference model — they take risks, and so do you. Maybe it's up to you to change paradigms first, and ideally before illness declares itself, to start thinking of yourself as a whole person before the Titans dismember and devour you.

Easier said than done. So how do you do it? Of course, there's no miracle solution to be learned in ten easy lessons. Once, my writer became ill and had to follow a strict diet, but his doctor told him: "Follow your instinct — your body knows what it needs and what it can't tolerate." That phrase stayed with him his entire life, and he made it a philosophy. As a cat, I know what I need, and sometimes I refuse salmon — even though I usually love it. I believe our organs send us signals when we ignore fads and friends' advice.

Of course, knowing your blood levels of carbohydrates and lipids can help you better understand what your body — and your mind — needs. In that realm, the signs are easier to decode. Avoid certain situations or people that make you feel uneasy. We cats are masters of avoidance. The moment a noise bothers us, we flee. As soon as something changes in the house, I go outside. When a person annoys me, I disappear. When the atmosphere displeases me, I avoid it. I am both very affectionate and antisocial. Maybe you can learn from my instinctive behavior.

But don't forget that I can spend long periods in near-total stillness. I'm there — sometimes lying down — but most often sitting, and I watch... no, I'm not really watching anything. I empty my mind. I'm simply present, and the outside world fades away. I no longer think. No images form in my little brain.

Let me tell you a few details about today. As usual, early this morning, I woke my friend. I went outside — my food is on the terrace. When he got up, I waited for him to sit in his armchair. It's true that I don't like to wait — I went out, came back... several times. I had gotten up full of energy, so when he finally came out to greet me, I played with him. In my excitement, I even bit the sleeves of his jacket. He then sat at the small table by the entrance. I climbed onto the blue pine tree across from the entrance, then came back down and sat not far from him — on the big black plastic bin. That's when I began what my writer calls my meditation... motionless... eyes fixed on the shrubs.

My friend was also relaxed; he was gazing straight ahead. We were in communion — without looking at each other. We were simply there... together. After that moment of tranquility, we each went on... to tend to our own business.

Chapter 9

Are We Communicating without Our Knowledge?

I think I got a little agitated by that Titans story. In fact, the mirror radiator right next to the entrance of the house now arouses a certain curiosity in me. Am I recognizing my image? Perhaps to recognize ourselves, the image we think we perceive in the mirror must first be dismembered into several facets, all these facets swallowed by the mirror to reveal only the core of our being, and it is through this heart that we will be able to communicate with humans, and humans with each other. This could lead us to believe that our heart continues to live in the hearts of the people who love us, that our heart survives our body, but also that a part of it remains hidden from us, a part that remains after the dismemberment of the mirror. My writer told me the story of a little girl who had drawn him twice, once with a big book next to a small black heart and once with a small book next to a big heart. He had to help her with her homework.

He told me about the aura, which is defined by the Larousse dictionary as an immaterial atmosphere that envelops or seems to envelop certain beings. Sometimes I only see a white dot just above the forehead, sometimes a black dot. I know I tend to run away when I see the latter. I like the idea of black photons studied at CERN in Geneva, since they would only be detected because the particle physicists are used to detecting black energy. Perhaps you feel that you lack energy when you are with certain people. My writer told me about a young patient whose mother suffered a severe depression after the birth of the child. This mother used to leave her daughter lying down and was only able to hold her when she was 3 years old. My writer sometimes emerges from these sessions in a state of great fatigue, as if he has exhausted all his energy, even though he feels the session went well. How can we understand this phenomenon? Obviously, this cannot be observed visually; we must trust what we feel, and it is also observable… subjectively. Let's trust our impressions, our sensations, our *visions*… we use this word to mean visualizing without necessarily seeing with our eyes. This can present itself as an image that comes to mind, a scene from your life that returns, a scenario constructed in the moment… so to each their own visions.

In his work, my writer is sensitive to the atmosphere, the ambiance, the spirit of the place when he works in an institution, in a group, of course with his patients, but also when he reads or when he listens to a speaker. It's true that in everyday life it would be hellish to decide at every moment who might give to us or who might take our energy. But let's not forget expressions like "sucking the air" or "sucking the marrow" out of something. Let's not be negative; there are also people who give us energy and people from whom we suck the air. My writer places me among the living beings who give more than they suck.

Let's go into more detail. He explained to me that in psychoanalysis it has often been thought that the patient transfers certain experiences, emotions, or feelings from their childhood onto the analyst. At first, the analyst occupies a neutral position, then begins to analyze what the patient has made them experience. I don't want to rehash the whole story. What I've understood is that now we're beginning to accept the idea that what happens in the session belongs to both participants and no longer just to the patient. My writer believes that most of the analysis happens without the knowledge of either speaker. This idea came to him while writing this book with me. Of course, he's the one writing; of course, he puts his own mind into it, he slips in his supposed knowledge, he observes me and thinks for me. But I believe that the path of our writing happens without our knowledge. I'll try to be clearer. Deep down, we communicate; don't ask me how — I don't know. We both know it's happening. I'm going to take another path, that of communication between two humans. Rationally, it is obvious that your communication takes place through your language, through the feelings you feel for each other — I don't want to give you the whole list... If I take the example of the little girl who only knew her mother's arms at the age of 3 and who provokes this feeling of exhaustion in her therapist, it is clear that during the session they exchange words and that he is happy with the progress this girl is making. But is this the essence of their communication? I don't think so. Does it happen without their knowledge? Yes, my writer may think that this girl is taking all the attention she didn't get as a baby. He might also think that this girl is unknowingly feeding off her therapist's life energy. Yes, but then, does this special attention nourish her, or will all of that be lost again when she leaves the therapy room? It's hard to answer. On the other hand, if he abandons this pattern and tells himself that something is built from the space they share, from being together, like invisible stitches that weave them together, without either of them knowing how, they would trust the fact of being there, a bit like my writer and I when we are a little distance apart in silence. But for that, we must abandon the idea of an interrelation, of a relationship between one and the other, and venture into another geometry, a geometry where we would no longer be in a space that separates us or that we must travel through to reach the other. It would be a dimensionless, immediate space, where points coincide, where our minds meet in an instantaneous here and now, being there without seeing, without thinking, without feeling — all of this will come later, like successive layers that would be born from this first silent encounter. And I believe that these ideas that seem crazy to humans, my writer draws them from our primordial making – that means that they exist from the beginning. How do you think the first humans communicated? By gestures? But before gestures? By shouts? And before shouts? It would be a kind of big bang of communication, but not an explosion, rather a great silence, a direct experience of the other.

Chapter 10

Between Being and Knowing

Who said we are within ourselves? Of course, this belief is necessary — just as it's necessary for the experimenter to believe that the phenomenon they are observing is outside themselves. Without this, we'd all fall into deep confusion and lose our sense of existing and of thinking about the world.

This is where a cat's opinion becomes important.

I don't think I have the feeling of existing — nor even the capacity to think. I am in the world without being able to represent it. As I've already said, my perception is direct. At most, my memory isn't about storing information but retrieving a perception. My sense of existing isn't individualized. That is, I can't say to myself, "I am a cat," or "I'm going to do this or that." And yet I experience pleasure and have desires. I feel pleasure when I'm on my friend's lap, when he opens those little cans with finely crushed fish, when I run to him after my morning walk, when I stretch my whole body, or when I meditate in silence.

Yes, I have desires — even if I can't articulate them. I can express the desire to go outside, the desire for my writer to sit in his armchair, the desire for milk, or for him to show me how to climb down from the living-room beams using the ladder that leans against the wall. I have desires and pleasure directly — without knowing that I have them.

You, on the other hand, know that you have them... well, not always, because sometimes they're unconscious. I might say that you believe you're conscious of being conscious, while I'm not even unconscious of being unconscious. (I'm joking!) Either way, your system of representation keeps you from being fully in the world, while my direct way of living doesn't allow me to represent it.

So the question arises differently for you and for me. You *think* you are, while I *am* — without knowing it. That's why the dialogue between my writer and me is important. It helps him be a little more, and helps me know a little more. It brings him more into the world, and gives me a touch more distance from it.

Lately, he has realized that he prefers writing when I'm not there — favoring a kind of mind-to-mind communication and simply being with me, without writing, when we're in close contact. Of course, when I sleep on his lap, he writes, because he believes many ideas come to him during my sleep. We follow opposite but complementary paths.

His path involves breaking the mirror's reflection — what he thinks he is — to access what he really experiences, to simply be there. My path involves letting go of the feeling of being one with everything, of being merged with the world, in order to construct an image of myself as a distinct figure. I search for this in the kitchen mirror. He searches by listening to his vague impressions, by daring to step outside the standard model — to borrow a term dear to particle physicists.

Let's return to those who deposit things in us they don't want to keep, or who absorb our vital energy.

Let's start with my writer and me. He would like to free himself from overly rational thinking to liberate his mind. I would like to get rid of the panicky anxiety that overtakes me whenever something in the house changes. He wants to think freely, outside the model proposed by the multitude — by "the many," as Heraclitus said. I want to see a world that flows continuously instead of appearing in scattered dots. He wants to discover other dimensions within the space that surrounds him.

However, if I take too geometric a path, he'll lose the inspiration that guides him off the beaten track. And if he ventures too far into the darkness, I might lose my grip on reality. We are condemned to think together.

But I believe we've plunged into grand theory to avoid dealing with the original question — of depositing or dispossession. We could frame it differently: What is placed within us, and what is taken from us?

But first, we need to clarify who or what this "we" is. Let's not go in circles! We come back to the undecidability in Schrödinger's cat experiment. To say "we" is to open the box and decide who or what we are. If we leave the box closed, we remain free to become — without deciding in advance. In that case, "we" would no longer mean anything; nor would "I."

I find that my writer goes too far, and in the end, nothing remains — only an uncertain becoming, an unknown path. That's why he replaces the word "unconscious" with "unknowing," since the unconscious implies something within us, while unknowing stirs curiosity toward the unknown.

In the world of elementary particles, black photons absorb energy, while the Higgs boson gives mass to particles — hence its nickname, the "God particle."

I know — it's hard to follow our wild ideas. So I asked my writer to give an example — like that of his little patient, the one who seemed to absorb his energy.

In fact, he has just had a session with her. This time, she crouched at the back of the room, as if closing herself off from all communication. He tried to tell her that she was reliving her earliest days, when her mother could only meet her basic needs, unable to hold her. No reaction.

He then remembered something — how once, when he got up from his chair to look at a drawing she was making on the board, she exclaimed: "Ah, you're alive! I thought you were a ghost."

He then rose again and sat beside her. He spoke gently, reminding her of that ghost story, and suggesting that perhaps, when she was very little, her mother had seemed like a ghost. She emerged from her bubble and began speaking to him softly, with joy.

So why the exhaustion that struck him after their previous session? Had he found himself taking the ghost's place? Had her withdrawal disturbed the space of the session – creating a kind of black hole that absorbed part of the room? Could the atmosphere of a session be like the spirit of the place? Could that spirit be subject to turbulence, to disturbances left behind by other patients?

In that case, the session room would not be a sacred temple but a living space – one where visitors leave traces. We might then find ourselves dealing with material that cannot be reduced to fantasy but instead consists of impressions from the past that transcend time – no, that are present, or made present – as though past and present were one.

Wow, what a long monologue! We've wandered all this way, forgetting the original question. But was there ever a beginning? Maybe we'll encounter it again along the way.

Chapter 11

Incorporating the World?

After this marathon, I felt like resting under my favorite tree. From there, I can see the house and stay connected to the green of the ground and the blue of the sky. I can free myself from all the questions that torment my writer's mind — not mine. Here, there are no spatiotemporal disturbances. Here, a tree is a tree, and I don't need to know or speak that word. I simply feel good and breathe easily, far from all the mental burdens he places on me — yet another example of how he deposits some of his concerns within me. And then it's up to me to detox from it all.

Of course, the ghost story interests me, and I enjoy it when he talks to me about his work. But I think he sometimes overdoes his explanations. I'm going to fall asleep now, in the shade of this old oak tree — that's its name — hoping to have some new visions.

The image of the oak lingers in my sleep. I see the sky through its foliage, as if green and blue were sharing the space. But this two-toned space forms a particular shape, a shape that moves — there's a light breeze — shifting its colors not across a surface but within a hemisphere. This hemisphere transforms into a giant magnifying glass that absorbs the foliage, the branches, and even the entire trunk. I feel myself being pulled upward, as if everything is converging into this concave figure. And to my amazement, I realize I am inside my eye — an eye absorbing all my energy.

My writer believes my sensoriality is evolving, that my vision — my sensory vision — is overtaking my other senses. My vision reveals that seeing isn't only about grasping an object outside ourselves but also about the outside world being absorbed by our eye — incorporated. It may sound like a banality, but if we absorb the external world without remaining separate from it, then we are, in part, made up of what surrounds us. We could say: the world is in us.

And that, of course, changes our relationship to it. It's like when we say that the observer is part of the phenomenon they study. Maybe this is a further step toward a Copernican revolution: the world doesn't revolve around us — we revolve around the world.

But it's easy to say "the world," or even "the external world." What is the world, really? A vast question.

Let's try to organize things a bit. First, there is what we might call the world of reality — a continuous space through which we can move from one point to another along a measurable path. It's the universe of measurements, in three dimensions. With the notion of time, things get more complicated, since our subjective experience of time shifts depending on the situation and doesn't always match the ticking of seconds. If you look closely, you'll notice that the space we travel feels different depending on whether we walk, ride a train, or fly. But meters and minutes are there to reassure us that all of it is stable. Basic geometry also comforts us, since everything can be reduced to lines, surfaces, and volumes.

Only the point poses a problem — it has no dimensions. And no matter how many billions of points you align, you'll never get a segment... unless maybe to infinity. But once you speak of infinity, you've already left the world of measurable dimensions.

As we've already said, in the infinitely small and the infinitely large, things shift. In the first, space might be made of tiny grains, like pixels (see the work of Carlo Rovelli). Or of a supersymmetry that predicts a partner particle for every known one, to explain where mass comes from.

In the infinitely large, things are also complex. A British physicist, Paul Dirac, once proposed that for every particle, there is a corresponding antiparticle, identical in every way except for its charge. For example, for every electron, there must be a positron — an antielectron — with the same properties but a positive charge. This idea made it possible to imagine galaxies and even entire universes made of antimatter.

Clearly, all of this goes far beyond what I can truly grasp of these theories. Readers who feel the same might be wise to skip that last page. Still, these ideas resonate with my daily experiences.

Here, we step beyond the world of measurements and into other realities — just like physicists who show us other possible spaces.

For me, the house and the small forest are two different worlds. The house is a closed space, made by humans. I'm no longer in direct contact with the earth or the sky. I have to adapt, create new parameters. It's a bit like what humans have done ever since they first sought shelter from nature — first in caves, and later in constructed enclosures. But humans didn't stop there. They did the same thing with their thoughts: they built models to understand nature.

All of this is to say that when I'm in the small forest, I return to my primal instincts. But in the house, I have to completely shift my sense of the world. It took humans tens of thousands of years to transition from the outside to the inside. Inside, all these objects mean nothing to me. They were manufactured — I can't see their use.

And humans haven't just sheltered themselves from nature — they've invaded it, building ever-larger cities. Can we say the same of theoretical constructs? That they lock nature inside laboratories?

Yes and no.

Yes, because what we observe depends on our measuring instruments. Yes, because nature might otherwise be unobservable. Yes, because nature's signs might be indecipherable. Yes, because we are part of the phenomena we seek to observe.

But also no. No, because we can't escape our sensory reality. No, because we must believe it exists, somewhere.

So what is nature?

Nature is what falls... under our senses. We see rocks, trees, animals. We see the sky, the sea, and a piece of our Earth. Beyond our Earth, we observe galaxies. And beyond galaxies?

Beyond the visible, we must construct hypotheses: dark matter, unknown particles, gravitational waves...

What scientists observe keeps changing, as their instruments grow more precise. We might say that nature itself is always changing. It does not exist once and for all. And since we are part of what is observed, it and we change — perhaps not symmetrically.

In this way, nature never fully reveals itself, and we find ourselves in a probabilistic, rather than deterministic, perspective. Thus, we remain before Schrödinger's closed box, unsure whether to open it and collapse the phenomenon — or to remain in doubt.

As for me, I don't feel like I'm looking at nature from outside. I'm in it. I am one with it. And as my vision of the hemisphere shows, my eye absorbs and incorporates it. At the same time, I am pulled into it — just like my favorite tree.

And a cat's eye sees in its own way. I am one with nature in a way that is different from a bird, a fish, or an insect.

Peter Wohlleben's *The Hidden Life of Trees* shows us that trees speak to one another, share the riches of the soil, help one another, and learn together. And what of nature's riches? Are the soil, the waters, and the air part of nature?

Yes. Ancient philosophers spoke of four elements: earth, air, fire, and water. Some may see this as primitive pre-chemistry, something long surpassed. But listen to this passage from Empedocles — a Greek philosopher, poet, and physician from fifth-century Sicily:

> But come, hearken to my words, for it is learning that increaseth wisdom. As I said before, when I declared the heads of my discourse, I shall tell thee a twofold tale. At one time it grew together to be one only out of many, at another it parted asunder so as to be many instead of one: Fire and Water and Earth and the mighty height of Air; dread Strife, too, apart from these, of equal weight to each, and Love in their midst, equal in length and breadth. Her do thou contemplate with thy mind, nor sit with dazed eyes. It is she that is known as being implanted in the frame of mortals. It is she that makes them have thoughts of love and work the works of peace. They call her by the names of Joy and Aphrodite.

I love when my writer teaches me these stories from antiquity. It's as if something ancient resonates in my mind. I may not have self-consciousness, but I have a mind. What I feel is this: we must experience the four elements directly.

It is by allowing ourselves to be absorbed by these elements — and by absorbing them — that our spirit grows richer. Perhaps this also means that if we stop measuring, classifying, and placing ourselves at the center of nature, we can enrich ourselves by becoming one with the four elements. One — as in unifying them into a whole.

What the ancients called "ether" is the fifth element — represented by the dodecahedron.

And here is also the song of the four elements. We haven't found its original source:

> Fire my Spirit
> Air my Breath
> Water my Blood
> Earth my Body

Chapter 12

Are We Carried by Nature?

With that final poetic flight, I felt as if I were floating in the air, as if my mind were on fire, as if my blood flowed like a river, as if my body were the earth. I was traversed by the four elements, and I felt in harmony with nature — superimposed upon it. This also sparked fear in me: fear of losing myself within these elements, fear of not being able to unify the many, fear of falling apart. But I also feel my being shifting — that I must allow myself to be carried by changing impressions. I'm caught in a circular motion, as if I must follow the various facets of nature, the 12 pentagonal faces of the dodecahedron, to find the unity of the sphere, like in my writer's dream.

I sense that my writer is completely lost. For once, he's the one who must follow me in my lucubrations. Here, he can no longer rely on his supposed knowledge. Here, he realizes that I am carried by nature — and that all his attempts to understand will be in vain. He realizes that it's one thing to use thought, another to let oneself be carried by it. That there's a difference between perceiving the world through one's senses and wandering through the drift of one's thoughts — straying from where one is meant to be.

He tries to reason, to cling to science and philosophy, but perhaps he must accept that when we stop viewing nature as something outside ourselves, we are swept into a whirlwind, losing our four cardinal points and carried instead by the four elements. Now I come back to earth, and perhaps he'll find some grounding in what he knows.

He dreamed of a problem: how to mix air with very fine dust. He visualized different combinations: the air and dust formed two separate clouds; they infiltrated each other; they flowed back and forth like the tide; they mixed until their individual properties were no longer distinguishable. When he woke, he imagined it as a dialogue between matter and non-matter. But how can we think about the immaterial?

Physics studies elementary particles — it assumes that new particles will continue to be discovered, such as those belonging to antimatter. Taking up my friend's dream as a metaphor, we could say that air and dust separated long ago: religious beliefs took on the air, science the dust. And so, for science, we might say, "Beyond this point, your ticket is no longer valid," meaning it can study particles in the air but not what the air contains.

But what is in the air? Thought, intuition, inspiration? Yes — but not only that. Also, the spirit of place, the spirit of the times, a state of mind. Yes: a state of mind. We might say that it's the current condition of our spirit. But is it even accurate to call it our spirit? Could it be a sort of breath of nature?

No — not only that. Since humans began organizing nature, classifying its elements, they introduced changes. They built societies, created governments, social and political structures... Spirit might be all of that — everything we breathe, the atmosphere of a country, and, of course, the spirit of the times: wars, terrorism...

In this sense, a state of mind could be defined as the condition of the moment. Maybe that's what happens during an intuition: a collapse, a sudden condensation of something that was in the air. Humans might act like lightning rods, giving form to the thoughts that hover in the atmosphere. They would be shaped by everything in the air — and this would shift their position, removing them from the center of the world. They would come to occupy a new place within nature — one equal to the other kingdoms: mineral, plant, animal — losing their supremacy.

At this point, I think my writer is overdoing it. Does he really want to go back to a time before the cave age? Before humans sheltered in homes, before civilization?

What I understand is that he's perhaps too influenced by ancient thought, by mythology, by a time when humanity depended on the whims — good or bad — of the gods of Olympus or those who dwelled in Tartarus.

Phew! I feel exhausted. My writer took a break before his brain caught fire, before it flew away on improbable winds, before it was swept by a river's current or buried in the depths of the earth.

He went out into the garden. I ran to him and lay on my back so he could play with me. He walked through the small forest and stopped near me. I rubbed against his legs again and again, even lay on his feet — to bring him back to earth. He had gone too far in his thoughts, and I wanted to show him that real wisdom lies in simply being present.

I sat between two trees, still, with my gaze fixed. He came toward me. He was struck by my stillness. He walked a little farther. I know he watched me, not without anxiety. He was relieved when he saw me move, exploring the grass that opened before me. He returned to his armchair to write. I went into the house, meowed to let him know I was with him, curled up on his lap for a few minutes, and then left again — returning to that same spot between the two trees, in the same motionless pose.

A strange idea crossed his mind: that this precise spot might be the place I would choose to die. It's a sad thought, and I wonder if writing about me all the time isn't becoming too much for him. It's terrible — all the mental architecture he must build to describe what is simply natural to me. I think humans torture themselves with their thoughts. I believe they pay dearly for having secondary consciousness. Watching how they exhaust themselves thinking, I feel lucky to live the way I do. And maybe — just maybe — if we cats could share our way of thinking, humans might stop looking down on us.

Now I'm back on his lap, performing my ablutions, as he calls them — cleansing both body and mind. I have a question:

what if all this writing is really just a way of asking me to strip him of the overwhelming complexity of his mind? What if I were a kind of master to him, teaching him how to be Zen, as I am?

It's true that it goes both ways. Not long ago, he helped calm my fear of shadows. We are like communicating vessels — he calls it "homeostasis." Obviously, I don't have access to everything he can learn from books. But he doesn't have the chance to live in the world as directly as I do.

Whenever I see him, it's like reuniting with a long-lost friend — even if I had only just left his side. Every time we meet, it feels new: I run to him, rub against his legs, then sit quietly nearby. But this happens only in a certain area — mainly on the terrace off the living room, and sometimes in the small forest that stretches beyond it. I occasionally follow him around the other side of the house, along the path that runs by the pond and fields.

For me, it's like what you feel when something or someone draws you in — a landscape or a person who captures your attention. I am attached to him, and this attachment has become exclusive. He is my only human — and perhaps the only living being I acknowledge — since I ignore or chase away other cats who prowl near the house.

The animals in the forest, like squirrels, stir my curiosity — but I watch them discreetly. What I love about my writer is that he talks to me, kisses me, and calls me by nicknames. But don't think I'm only in it for affection. My desire to be near him goes both ways — I love giving him warmth, too.

But there's even more: I am highly attuned to his emotional state. It's as if I'm drawn to both his joys and his sadness. Both poles are equally endearing — the first to share in our well-being, the second to give him… yes, love. It's as if I must compensate for the negative in him with my total attention. When he's upset or angry, though, I tend to flee — perhaps because I experience his anger as an attack. I probably know how to give more than I know how to receive. I believe I only give positive things – and I manage my own negatives by sharpening my claws, climbing trees or ladders, racing around, but especially through ablution, rest, meditation, and as I said, by fleeing people or places that give off a negative energy.

Inside the house, my writer is the center of my world. Outside, he comes to visit me. The things inside the house don't interest me much – except for the pencils lying on the living-room table, which I enjoy batting from paw to paw. Obviously, the center of attraction is his armchair, especially his lap, or the edge of his bed near his pillow. If he moves in his sleep, then the big cushions on the sofa. Sometimes I explore to check for new objects – but otherwise, the interior doesn't concern me much.

On the other hand, I sometimes make my home in the barn or the old part of the mill – places not inhabited by humans – when he's away or it's too cold to sleep outdoors.

In my life with him, I experience our bond – my attachment to him, his love for me. Sometimes we are inseparable, tangled together. Other times, I sense a distance – for example, when I have to meow to get him to sit in his armchair or open the French doors. Maybe I'm learning that I exist.

All this is to say: we love each other, even without the ability to communicate through language. Lacking words, we've developed our own form of communication. When we're together, it's self-evident – though hard to describe. Perhaps it's like early humans, before they had gestures, back in the misty past before they took shelter in caves.

Besides, we know that even trees communicate, and that humans communicate far more than they realize. Even in the simplest geometry, two points might allow a straight line to be drawn – but two points next to each other can only be superimposed or joined by the line that connects them across a distance.

My writer began explaining something – something Zeno of Elea once proposed, and here is a fragment:

> You cannot cross an infinite number of points in a finite time. You must travel half the distance before you can travel the whole, and half of that half before that, and so on ad infinitum. Thus, there are an infinite number of points in any given space, and you cannot touch all of them, one after the other, in a finite time.

Chapter 13

Does Knowledge Defy the Passing of Time?

Last night, my writer dreamed — or rather, while sleeping, he saw a red stone, a regularly shaped, elongated figure, like a rectangular parallelepiped with 12 softened edges. It was the color that caught his eye more than the shape: a pure, almost scintillating red, radiant, as though it gave off luminous energy. Upon waking, he told himself that the dream followed naturally from our ongoing reflections about communicating across distance.

And now here is this red stone — perhaps a carnelian — and he's amused by the idea that if physicists believe dark matter and black photons absorb particle energy, then red matter — let's call them "red photons" — might release energy. So, black photons would be attractive or extractive, and red photons... well, let's call them "red dots," so as not to upset the physicists. Red dots would be...

We realize the antonym of "attractive" is "repulsive." But my writer searches for a word that suggests giving — not rejecting. Animating? Enlivening? No — those suggest movement or life. Generous? Maybe. Giving? Too vague. What if we said in love? Yes — red dots in love. That suits my way of loving him. Yes, giving him red dots. Love unites two beings; love connects us to nature. Love lets us commune with thinkers who lived 25 centuries ago. A black heart needs love; a red heart can give it.

It's like in diagrams of the circulation of blood: the blood that leaves the heart is drawn in red; the blood that returns, in a dark color. My writer wonders why he's so interested in ancient thinkers. Could it be that ancient philosophers are still communicating their thoughts to us?

When he was young, he once woke up with a word repeating itself in his mind: Empedocles. He figured he must have heard it in a philosophy class. Yes — but why did that name surface so vividly that morning?

You firmly believe you acquire knowledge from books, or from a teacher. It seems unthinkable that there could be other channels — for example, that the thoughts of the ancients might still be reaching us beyond historical record. We often speak of "thoughts in the air" — of their time. But what if some are outside of time?

Let's propose this — not to prove it but to open the door. Proof, explanation, demonstration: perhaps they only distance us from intuitive knowledge.

As a cat, I can prove nothing. But I can experience.

For instance, when I meow for my writer to open the door to the old bedroom where the former owners once slept, I feel something particular — as though I expect to see them. Some might say I remember their presence; others that I'm sensing traces they left behind.

But what if there were a memory without traces?

How do you explain ideas that come to you spontaneously? Or why new thoughts emerge during a conversation? My writer and I believe that by constantly explaining, observing, and theorizing, humans risk losing touch with much that is immaterial.

Thought is immaterial — it's a shame to reduce it to neural connections. The love we feel for a partner, a friend, a child — it crosses oceans, outlives time. We continue loving those who have passed. In other cultures, the dead still live among the living. People see them, talk to them.

Why not apply this to great thinkers of the past? Why would modern ones have replaced them?

There are two kinds of progress. The first is technological — undeniably advancing and improving our tools, our communication. Science progresses: mathematics, physics, astronomy, medicine — these fields move forward.

But the second idea of progress — progress of thought — may not be linear. It's not certain that today's philosophy is more advanced than that of antiquity. Nor that Socrates, Plato, or Aristotle surpassed the so-called pre-Socratic philosophers.

Thinkers like Anaximander, Pythagoras, Heraclitus, Parmenides, Empedocles...

Here, my writer launched into one of his usual rambles. But as for me, I bristle at another misunderstanding about progress. I don't believe humans sit at the pinnacle of evolution, having achieved some higher consciousness. Granted, I make exceptions for those who care about animals, plants — even stones.

But for most, our lives are seen as primitive, wild.

Once, my writer heard a philosopher say he'd speak with animals when they built libraries. Poor philosophy! I believe humans still have much to learn from us — if only they could build libraries out of pawprints, not just books.

That's why I feel closer to the philosophers of antiquity, who sought to reveal nature, not encase it in theory.

But let's come back to the love that crosses oceans — and defies time.

The word "philosophy" means "love of wisdom." It suggests that love leads us to knowledge. Could we say love carries us toward discovery?

On this point, my writer and I agree. He believes knowledge isn't locked away in libraries and that seeking it only in laboratories leads us astray.

We — not just I, as a cat, but all living beings — believe that we have access to knowledge long forgotten by humans in their so-called evolution.

Love is what unites. It opens us to the unknown. It's a dialogue with nature that defies rationality.

Love is not possession — it is discovery.

It's time for humans to revolve around the universe instead of always demanding that the universe revolve around them.

Last night, my writer and I both dreamed.

In my dream — more of an impression — a strong wind blew, preventing humans from closing doors and windows. Its force penetrated every space people had taken refuge in.

My writer's dream was apparently different. He lived in a large bungalow with two entrances. From the eastern entrance, he saw two police cars and officers heading toward the other side. Strangely, instead of walking through the house, he exited outside — and found himself in the Amazon rainforest. Everything was a deep, humid green. He had trouble following the trail, which formed only as he walked, camouflaged in the same green as the forest.

After much effort, he reached the other side. There, the police officers showed him a dead man, lying face down. He was told to identify the body. Someone gently lifted the stranger's head.

It was himself.

Apparently, the dreams have nothing in common. But let's overlap them.

In both, there's an interior and an exterior. In both, nature asserts itself. Both relate to our writing. In each, nature isn't hostile — but it disrupts all forms of closure.

In his, you must die — as an individual — to access greater knowledge. A Copernican revolution. A crossing from East to West, like Columbus. He even thinks of the Berlin Wall and the expression "to be in the West" — meaning madness or eccentricity.

Yes, you need to be a little mad to want to cross the wall… of rationality.

In my dream, which is more instinctive, human constructions are no longer sealed. The wind blows through, dismantling your convictions about "reality" — the world you sense through faculties that are not fixed or universal. Our faculties — those of animals — differ from yours. Why would your perception be the true one?

Besides, you've developed the habit of dismembering everything — just like the Titans did with Dionysus. You've cut space, split time, dissected the body into systems. Even your minds have been fragmented by psychologists into various parts.

You've lost the unity of the world — and of being.

Empedocles would say that divisive hate had triumphed over unifying love.

Phew! That felt good to get out.

But remember — after Dionysus's dismemberment, unity was rediscovered.

Maybe this is the lesson for Western medicine: to find unity again, after dissection.

Pythagoras called One the principle of all things. He called Two "matter," because it separates.

If we stay with One, we can keep loving our old loves — dead or alive. We can keep the great thinkers of history alive, instead of replacing them with the next trend.

All those writers, inventors, philosophers — may they rise again from the dust of libraries and live!

My writer told me about a book called *Fahrenheit 451* by Ray Bradbury. Published in 1953, it's a dystopia — a negative utopia — a vision of a world where human happiness depends entirely on screens. Books are banned, considered dangerous because they provoke unwanted feelings and thoughts.

The protagonist, Montag, is a fireman — not one who puts out fires but one who burns books.

There's also a film version, directed by François Truffaut.

What I loved most about the story is its ending — when a group of resistance fighters survive by reciting the great works of literature aloud.

Chapter 14

Seeing and Being

Let's clarify things a little. How many authors, how many researchers, how many philosophers have chosen two over one? We've defined an earthly world and a celestial world. We've often split the body from the mind, separated reality from imagination. Freud divided the individual into conscious and unconscious selves. For Descartes, the mind was an immaterial and indivisible substance, while the body was material and infinitely divisible.

It's true that once such divisions are made, rediscovering unity becomes difficult. And so, we search for interactions: the neural correlates of consciousness, the connections between the psychic and the somatic, between classical and quantum physics...

For me, things are perhaps simpler. My writer might have me say: I do not think, therefore I am. Because from the moment I think the world, I separate myself from it.

As far as I'm concerned, the question of whether cats recognize themselves in a mirror is meaningless. We have no image of ourselves. And do humans truly recognize themselves in a mirror?

Let's do a little exercise. When you wake up in the morning, try to feel your state of mind — then go to the bathroom and look at yourself in the mirror. Does the person you see match the one you felt you were?

I believe that upon waking, you are one. And once in front of the mirror, you become two.

Has the human eye introduced this separation?

Yes. Humans believe that what they see is outside themselves — and that what they see is real. We might say the world presents itself, while humans represent it. But presentation is, and representation is a construction — one shaped by the way the brain works.

You've trained your eye to be active, to capture objects. But the eye is also passive. It receives stimuli you cannot decode. And more than that — it cannot perceive everything.

Here's a question: would your sensory system, your brain, function differently if you hadn't trained your eye to try to put the world inside you?

Since Aristotle — who said that "the virtue of the eye makes both the eye and its function equally perfect, because it is through the eye that vision is completed in us as it should be" — you've considered vision your primary tool for understanding the world.

But before Aristotle?

Let's turn to Heraclitus: "Presumptuousness is a sacred disease, and sight is illusory ... Eyes and ears are bad witnesses for men if their souls do not understand their language."

I'll raise my paw — sorry, my hand.

Let's keep it simple. I exist in life without knowing it. You, on the other hand, know you're alive, yet you're not entirely in it.

As a cat, I make no distinction between seeing and being seen. I'm simply drawn toward good sensations and away from unpleasant ones. Don't think nature is always good. Like black photons that absorb energy from other particles, nature can either draw us in gently or absorb us destructively — love us like a starry sky or devour us like a black hole.

My writer and I believe that elementary particle physicists are opening fascinating paths for understanding the world. There are also scientists exploring multiverses, probabilistic grains of space, quantum entanglement, and nonlocal phenomena.

I was supposed to keep this simple — and I made it complicated.

All of this is to say: you must step outside the box you've trapped yourself in – your cranium. Stop clinging to your continuous, three-dimensional space. By structuring space this way, you've locked yourself into a model where what doesn't fit becomes invisible.

Let the irrational and intuitive breathe. Cultivate your imagination. Allow other visions of the world to exist – those that can't be measured. Accept that not everything is thinkable. Accept that your eye can be deceived.

Native American wisdom says love is like the wind: we can feel its effects, but we cannot see it. You can measure blood pressure, track brain activity – but love remains invisible and indivisible. It transcends reason. It defies measurement.

And what about hate?

Let's listen to Empedocles:

> For truly they [Love and Hate] were before time, and they will be; and never, I believe, will infinite time be empty of this couple ... The union of all things brings a generation into existence and destroys it; the other grows and dissipates when things separate ...

This gives rise to an idea between my writer and me: that we all live in two dimensions at once. One is the dimension of unity, where minds meet and become one. The other is that of division and separation: internal world and external world, body and mind, self and other.

Ask yourself this: why do couples who begin in love sometimes part in hatred?

Perhaps the real dimension – the spiritual one – becomes dissociated from everyday life. Isn't it often said that daily life kills love?

Of course, we can't live entirely in the "one." We cats have also constructed our own reality. We must juggle the two.

Our mind, our intuitions, our dreams — these unfold in the one. Our routines, logic, and moderation live in the two.

So keep dancing on both feet.

One foot alone will carry you into mysticism or madness. Two feet alone will cut you off from your inner life.

Then again... I have four legs.

Should I dance to a four-beat rhythm?

Chapter 15

We Live in Multiple Worlds

What if there were multiple dimensions?

I won't bore you with string theory — a unified theory of force fields and matter particles in the universe — which posits 11 dimensions, or with the Blue Brain Project, which discovered a multidimensional universe in our neural networks. That means our brains might not function solely within the usual three dimensions but could also operate within as many as 11.

And once again, my life as a cat might help illustrate this.

Take sensory processing, for instance. All your senses work in concert: an object that is seen, smelled, or touched is processed as a single thing, regardless of the sensory input. But for us, each sense opens up a different world. Add to that our whiskers, our fur, our tail...

All this is to say: for me, space has more than three dimensions.

Mentally, you too inhabit multiple dimensions. I'll just name a few: the dream world, distinct from the world of sleep; the world of your intuitions; the world of your thoughts. For me, all of this is compressed into a single whole. So there seems to be a kind of inverted symmetry between you and me: you compress spaces into one, and you differentiate mental dimensions. We, on the other hand, have a single mind — but our space divides into many dimensions.

Your structuring of the world has allowed you to build extraordinary things. Your technology has made huge leaps. Science has probed elementary particles and black holes; medicine now has sophisticated instruments. You can speak with each other and even see each other on your smartphones across thousands of kilometers.

As a cat, all this progress leaves me rather indifferent.

We carry nature within us — and perhaps one day that will be of use to you. Maybe you'll come to realize that by endlessly separating the infinitely small from the infinitely large, by multiplying medical specialties, by leaving to religion what you refused to contemplate, and by torturing nature with concrete — you have, through all this division and cutting, strayed further and further from unity.

From the Love of Empedocles, you've let Hate flood the world.

I got a little carried away there, but I'm happy that my writer can put these deep feelings into words.

And I must thank you — because you've always respected our autonomy. Unlike dogs, who've been bred to be useful to you, or livestock raised for food, or animals hunted as threats, no one asks us to work, perform tricks, or grow fat to be eaten. We are privileged. Humanity has left us in peace for millennia.

My writer even wonders whether, since the dawn of time, humans have deposited in us what they needed to abandon to keep pace with civilization. Like me, perhaps that early human didn't always sleep well. Maybe he began trying to control what frightened him — constructing representations to distance himself from the threatening world.

So maybe... we are the guardians of what humanity once was.

My writer dreamed — or more precisely, he saw, while asleep, the cover of an ancient book with golden embellishments. He thought it was an image from the Middle Ages, something like a religious icon. At the same time, he visualized a text on a computer screen. The text was cut in two, horizontally, as though trying to form itself clearly but unable to fully appear — still flickering, still unreadable.

Obviously, these two texts — the ancient and the modern — relate to our own writing, which explores both scientific discoveries and ancient thought. The divided, unreadable screen might represent our dialogue. But why the medieval icon?

It's true we've avoided religion in our conversations so far.

Perhaps the dream signals that it's time for my writer to open the Bible. Was the image a glimpse of Gutenberg's first printed edition? No — because what he saw had a sacred image, perhaps a Byzantine icon.

He once heard Jean-François Froger — a physicist, philosopher, and exegete — tell a story at a conference: While fasting for several days, Froger lent part of his house to a friend. They met just once a day for an hour to speak. During that fast, the friend had a vision of an icon. Years later, in a small town neither had ever visited, the friend felt an irresistible urge to enter a church. Inside, he found that very icon from his vision.

This morning, my writer recalled that story — it had deeply struck him before. But why did it resurface now, through the dream of an icon?

And why was the modern text split in two, flickering, struggling to form itself?

In a moment of mystical reflection, he thought maybe the dream was a sign, telling him that inspiration would come... from something beyond.

Then, he stopped thinking.

Of course, I've had no religious education, and I can't believe a higher power directs my intuitions. For me, intuition is fused with sensation. It's what I feel directly at any moment: an indescribable air, an immaterial atmosphere, an invisible pulse, a silent shift between light and shadow, a cloud of tiny specks...

... Red and black dots.

Maybe this intangible air is simply the dissolving of the boundary between human and world. When I say "world," I mean: nature, physis, the cosmos, the whole, the one, the *logos* — all words I've learned. But by naming them, we draw the boundary again.

Maybe, when we sleep, that boundary disappears. Maybe that's when intuition arises.

The Greek word *alētheia* — often translated as "truth" — actually means "unveiling."

Yes: to unveil what cannot be seen with the senses. To go beyond material reality.

Last night, my writer dreamed again.

He saw a very tall figure, twice his height, wearing a long black robe. Was it a priest? A shaman? A medieval figure? The robe bore golden patterns, like the icon in the previous dream. Its embroidery was blurred — like the old book cover, like the split text that never fully formed.

This tall figure seemed to be wondering how to board a plane.

At that point, I couldn't follow him anymore.

Is he discovering a new part of himself? Is a new path opening? Is he drifting toward mystical landscapes?

I'll try to bring him back to earth.

Yes, our writing occupies his thoughts deeply — the size of the figure in the dream. Yes, when he opens his tablet, he doesn't yet know what will take shape on the screen — like the blurred writing in his dream. Yes, maybe he's wondering whether he can handle everything he's trying to cover — ancient thought, quantum physics, all these dimensions...

Thankfully, I'm here to remind him: when you try to explain everything, you fall into the trap of over-rationality — exactly what we're trying to critique.

He needs to relax. He can watch me doze on the terrace.

I'm not preoccupied with golden, Byzantine, or mystical icons. I'm here, in the immediacy of things — without agenda, without calculation.

But maybe my writer is showing me how complicated human life has become — ever since humans acquired the ability to think.

That's one of his struggles: being forced to think about life, instead of just living it.

He should follow my example.

I live — without being able to think about living.

Chapter 16

The Spirit Is Not Measured by the Mind

But what drove human beings to leave their primitive environment to build an increasingly complex civilization? And why have we animals not changed our way of life?

Well, that's not entirely true — some of us have changed, adapting to the intrusion of your constructions into our habitats. Others have disappeared entirely. So sometimes, while believing they are building, humans destroy. They wanted to conquer nature, understand it, classify it... But do they destroy nature in order to better understand it?

Then there's the supremacy that some of you exhibit toward us. You think you're superior — at the top of the animal kingdom. You claim your brains are more developed than ours.

We remain part of nature, while you've become part of culture — a culture you've sometimes constructed artificially, and often at the expense of natural resources. For example, in pharmacology, you've synthesized certain molecules based on what you found in plants. Do you want to do the same with nature as a whole?

But I'm getting carried away.

Now it's my writer's turn to balance things. He believes not everything is negative about your civilization's progress. Certainly, you've moved away from direct contact with nature — but in doing so, you've opened many doors to new knowledge. Your curiosity has enabled you to make infinite discoveries. Research expands every day into uncharted territory.

It's true — we cats aren't interested in our history, we have no libraries, we don't read. But we carry history in another way: we carry it in silence. Our thoughts are so free we can't even formulate them — they are self-evident. For you, free thought is often masked by social conventions, though sometimes you still feel it without knowing why.

Yes, we've spoken of communication from unconscious to unconscious. But we prefer to speak of communication from mind to mind. And the mind is not something to be measured — it *is*.

Let's take it a step further — just for fun: does a pebble have a mind?

But to say it "has" a mind is already to attribute something to it. No — the pebble doesn't have a mind. It is.

Let me come back down to earth. Enough theorizing about the mind.

This morning, I gently placed one paw on my writer's shoulder. He woke with a jolt, flailing his arms as if fending off an attacker. Once awake, he realized I just wanted to go outside.

But where had he been during his sleep?

Maybe it's time to rethink our nights — not just as pauses punctuated by dreams about yesterday's worries or childhood echoes. Where are we when we sleep?

I sleep all the time. I know I exist in another dimension. It's hard to explain, but that dimension stays with me, even when I'm awake.

Let's consider something simple: difficulty falling asleep. Perhaps insomnia reveals how hard it can be to travel into the realm of sleep. I spend most of my life dozing. For me, sleep is my main world. For you, it's the reverse — sleep remains a mystery.

Now, consider these two expressions: "Night brings counsel" and "Let sleeping cats lie."

The first suggests that night brings wisdom. The second — my writer taught me — has ancient roots in Old French: *Ne ramentevez point le chat qui dort*. The verb *ramentever* means "to recall," "to remember." So maybe the saying originally meant: don't remember what happens in sleep.

Perhaps sleep grants access to a world that must be forgotten upon waking. The ancients believed that souls, before leaving the Underworld, had to drink from the River Lethe, which erased memory. (*Alētheia* – Greek for truth – literally means "un-forgetting.")

Here are some verses from Baudelaire on Lethe:

I want to sleep! To sleep rather than live!
In a sleep as sweet as death ...

To drown my calmed sobs
Nothing beats the abyss of your bed;
Powerful oblivion dwells on your lips,
And Lethe flows in your kisses.

Can we imagine crossing that river both ways?

In one direction, we forget what we've seen in sleep. In the other, we leave waking reality to enter a dimension of pure consciousness, a direct awareness of a world that escapes us while awake.

But we forgot the second expression – ah yes, night brings counsel. This saying carries us into a realm of wisdom and intuition. Here, we don't abandon the body to enter silent abstraction; we receive guidance and peace. We don't have to believe in Plato's realm of ideas – but perhaps sleep brings us into unity with ancient wisdom. And in this dimensionless world, words like "before" or "after" lose all meaning – there's no time, no space.

Maybe, following Empedocles, we could say that in sleep we are one – and that waking is the moment we become many, a dismembering of the self. Could sleep disorders be rooted in the fear of losing that unity? Is insomnia our attempt to control the pieces we must keep together while awake?

Because if we venture into sleep while already fragmented, the result might be a kind of inner catastrophe.

My writer and I talked about how we communicate – so that he could put into words what I feel. We spoke of a communication beyond space, a communication between minds.

That would mean a kind of instant connection – no travel, no medium. It just happens.

We believe human beings live in two dimensions. The first is the world of the observable – what you can see, measure, experience. The second is dimensionless. It might sound like a paradox or a riddle. But let's return to geometry for a moment.

A point has no dimension. And no matter how many points you collect, you'll never make a line – unless you imagine one. Yet you can type a point on your keyboard. You can draw one.

But the moment you do, it leaves the dimensionless and becomes part of real space.

Now consider thought.

Plato placed it in the world of Ideas. Some neuroscientists locate it in neurons. Others, in symbolic representation. Others still, in higher-order consciousness.

We cats? We think in a free way. A thought with no image. A fluid, immediate thought. A kind of pure thought – like the one humans touch during deep meditation. A thought without an object.

Empedocles believed that good thought aligns with the wisdom of nature. Bad thought arises from turning away from it. He wrote:

> For the wisdom of men grows according to what is before them.
> Out of these all things are formed and fitted together.
> By these do men think and feel pleasure and pain.

Let me try to explain how I see all this.

When I look at something, it presents itself to me.

My writer explained that Freud used the word *Vorstellung* — "presentation" — but French translators mistakenly rendered it as "représentation," with its mental connotation. That changed much of the original theory.

It's not the same to say something presents itself as to say we represent it. The meanings are almost opposite.

English translations kept the term "presentation." Freud believed presentation was fundamental — it creates the psyche. He saw it as the engine of thought.

Once again, my writer has gotten carried away with all his knowledge.

But what he means is this: it's nature that gives rise to the human as a thinking being — not the other way around.

Am I more complicated than he is?

Let me give you an example.

Often, I feel like the thing I'm perceiving is looking at me. You think you're seeing something outside yourself. I feel like the object strikes my gaze. As if it changes me.

You, on the other hand, filter the object through the image your brain has already formed of it.

When will you stop believing that what you see is necessarily real? That what you see is truth?

Ah! Now I'm getting carried away too.

But yes — we defend the wisdom of nature against the arrogance of the eye that claims to observe it.

Let nature look at us.

This is the riddle the Sphinx presented to Oedipus:

> At dawn, he crawls on four feet; at noon, he walks on two;
> in the evening, he staggers on three.
> What is this being — never the same, yet never many, always one?

There are several versions of this riddle. Here's another:

> What is the being that sometimes walks on four legs, sometimes on two, and sometimes on three?

Let's begin with the first version. The riddle is deliberately obscure. Its meaning isn't immediately clear. What is obvious is that a human being moves from infancy — crawling on all fours — to adulthood — walking upright — and finally to old age — leaning on a cane.

But this version also speaks of dawn, noon, and evening. So the riddle invokes the sun — its rise, its zenith, and its setting. Something is born from darkness, lives in light, and returns to darkness.

Are we never the same from day to day, from night to night — and yet still one?

Are we the same in waking as we are in sleep?

Dawn — this fragile moment when night hasn't fully departed and day opens its first eye — is my favorite time. I often wake my writer then so he'll let me out. I have the feeling that nature is still hesitant. Its shapes are dim, its presence is gentle, not yet insisting on my gaze.

At midday, the sun sharpens nature's features. Everything becomes more defined, more insistent. In the evening, when night falls, I enter a different kind of reality. Even if I feel comfortable in darkness, the shadows of night and the shadows of sleep tend to blend.

By solving the riddle, Oedipus escaped the abyss into which the Sphinx threw herself. But perhaps if he had dared to descend into the abyss of himself — if he had accepted being reborn again and again, to never remain the same — he might have avoided his own downfall.

If he had embraced the idea of never being the same without needing to be many, he might have relinquished the arrogance of trying to know the truth at all costs. He sought truth because he couldn't bear to doubt himself. He might have questioned whether he had indeed killed that man at the crossroads of the three paths. He might have seen that the Sphinx's riddle was about him — first and foremost.

Jocasta tried to temper his hunger for truth:

> What does a mortal have to fear — mere playthings of fate — when nothing can be known for sure? To live as one can, by chance, is by far the best.

My writer shared a literal translation of the riddle with me:

> What being —
> who has a voice,
> has four legs,
> then two legs,
> then three — does he become?

This version is more enigmatic. It speaks of voice and becoming. Everyone interprets it differently, but for us, the words "voice" and "become" struck deeply.

Could this be about a being who speaks — and becomes?

Could it be about living according to one's own voice, while also being shaped by destiny? About finding one's voice — and being spoken to?

But why four, two, three?

Let's also look at Oedipus's answer, again literally translated:

> What is said
> man
> be.

Here, being stands in contrast to becoming in the Sphinx's question. Oedipus confronts existence itself — existing in spite of what has been said, finding his own voice despite the prophecy.

And that is the tragedy: his parents wanted him dead, his baby feet pierced and bound. When he left the people he believed were his parents, he thought he was escaping fate — choosing his own path. But fate caught up with him. His entire life unraveled, taking him right back to that fateful crossroads, to the murder of his father.

After the death of his adoptive father, the king of Corinth, Oedipus could have succeeded him peacefully. But between a loving adoptive couple and a murderous biological one, he chose the latter.

He didn't kill himself. Instead, he blinded himself and said:

> As for me, as long as I live, may I never dwell in this city, the city of my fathers. Rather, let me live in the mountains, in Cithaeron, the place my parents had marked for my death — my grave before I ever drew breath. I'll die there, as they intended.

Why does my writer tell you this story?

Because he believes it reminds us that every human is born carrying the wishes of their parents — sometimes contradictory ones. Desires for repair, for continuity, for healing, or even to replace someone lost.

He once told me about two young patients, both born after the death of an older sibling. One child was given the same name as the deceased. The other was given a different name.

The second child's therapy lasted several years and allowed him to build an identity distinct from that of his lost sibling. For the first, however, her parents abruptly stopped the therapy, saying: "You want us to believe there are two children. But for us, there's only one."

They even took the child — which one? — to visit the grave of the sibling who bore her name.

Another patient, a young girl, spent her entire therapy filled with rage toward my writer. Her older sister had died in an accident. At the end of therapy, she told him her rage had been proportional to the love she felt for him. When she was 5, she said, she had considered jumping off the school roof because her parents only had eyes for her dead sister.

As with the riddle of the Sphinx — must we find our own voice to become something other than what's been said about us?

All of this is a bit much for me. We cats don't desire our kittens beforehand. But once they arrive, we love them with our whole body and soul — even if humans sometimes kill our young, often without remorse.

We aren't desired by our parents — but we are desired by humans. And their love matters greatly to us. Since ancient Egypt, they've protected us. We are enigmatic beings to you. And perhaps we inspire you to think differently about your own life and thoughts.

We like being with you, quietly watching you live.

My writer never wanted me to exist. I simply appeared one day at the mill he'd just bought. We learned to love each other. We became inseparable — even though his work takes him away during the week. The distance taught us to communicate differently.

That's how we discovered this dimensionless dimension — a world beyond measurement, beyond clocks. A world of immediacy. Of pure, primary consciousness.

With him, I am transformed — because I feel the love he has for me. I encounter a gaze different from the one nature gave me.

With me, he discovers a new way of thinking. He becomes sensitive to the imperceptible, to communication without images or words.

What astonishes him is that we cats are still the same as we were 3000 years ago. Humans, on the other hand, believe they've changed, that they've evolved...

Yes, their technology has transformed their daily reality. But has it changed the way they think? The way they love? The way they hate?

Certainly, human beings have made progress in the realm of measurement — they can count in light-years, detect subatomic particles, deduce the presence of dark photons. They can measure color, sound, even scent. They have discovered bacteria and viruses, and found remedies for disease.

But maybe, in doing so, they have drifted away from the love of wisdom — from the first philosophers. They no longer think about the invisible, except through what religion prescribes.

Humans have become like Saint Thomas: they must see to believe. They must prove — scientifically.

And in doing so, they may have lost sight of all that is not material, neural, genetic, or logical.

Chapter 17

Thinking without Ulterior Thoughts

This morning, my writer woke up with the word "think."

Thought is immaterial. It ignores space and time. It spans millennia. Sometimes, it floats in the air. And it belongs to no one.

As a cat, I think without necessarily having thoughts. My thought is free. It's a path without signposts. Like a river current, it flows, sometimes deviating from its course, sometimes drying up or flooding its banks.

I think and I am — without knowing that I think or that I am.

For me, thinking is an activity without ulterior motives. In that spirit, my writer read me a few verses by Parmenides — the poet, he emphasized, not the Plato character of the same name. "Come on, I'll tell you. You'll hear what Parmenides says are the only paths open to intelligence:

> 'You cannot have knowledge of what is not, you cannot grasp it or express it,
> because thought and being are one and the same thing.
> It doesn't matter to me whether I start on one side or the other;
> for in any case, I will retrace my steps.'"

I'm happy to hear this philosopher's words. I, too, think as I walk, and my wanderings reflect the rhythm of my thought. My thoughts have no goal — but I retrace my steps. My thought has no images — but I find my favorite spots, I relax, and I meditate. For me, that's thinking without thinking about anything.

Yes, thought and being are one and the same — though it's just a way of speaking. Thought and being aren't "things."

There are people who lose their memory. It's an illness. They think without images, without memory. They don't remember what they just did; they no longer recognize the people they love. But where are they, then?

Maybe they're nowhere. Maybe they simply are, without memory or direction.

I have many questions. Okay, yes — free thought without memory or purpose — but does what you think belong to you?

Is thought a private activity?

Certainly, my writer and I think differently. I think freely, directly. He is often weighed down by his supposed knowledge. And he must shape our thoughts — because he has to translate them into words, into something readable, maybe even understandable.

But where does thought come from?

Does it form only as it happens?

There are many paths here. First, we must ask: Are we talking about thinking in words? In images? Or of a pure thinking — without content?

What would contentless thought even be?

A current that flows freely — like energy without resistance? Like the flow of nervous circuits in the brain? According to Rodolfo Llinás, our neurons don't just communicate through synapses; they also bring together different electrical excitations from across the brain, creating wave-like configurations that surf over neuronal connections.

He believes the peaks of these waves create a zone of thought beyond consciousness: ideas not yet formulated, images not yet formed — a future not yet realized.

A virtual possibility — open to development. A window into complexity arising from simplicity.

That's when my writer's quotes usually begin to float over my head. But let me try to translate in my own way.

I think Llinás has perfectly described my kind of thinking. Thought without form. A virtual thought, open to infinite shapes.

Maybe my writer's job is to give shape to my as-yet-unformed ideas. And once he does, I can tell whether they resonate with me.

In this case, Llinás's formulation suits me. Even if my thought lacks precise form, it becomes clearer through my writer's.

That's the beauty of our dialogue. I carry primary thought, and it's through this that my writer dares to imagine a world without measure.

He explained to me that Freud's theories can be read in different ways. Let's keep it simple and focus on two.

In the first view, thought is formed from excitations – impulses that move through the body. In 1895 and 1896, Freud imagined three types of neurons:

- Permeable neurons, which let the excitation pass freely;
- Impermeable neurons, which absorb the excitation and create the first psychic traces;
- Perceptive neurons, which read the traces and create a second level of awareness.

Let me translate that into my own feline understanding:

When I perceive something, it either penetrates directly – without leaving a mark – or it carves out a trace.

These traces then become images, and eventually, for humans, words.

I don't have access to words. And my images exist only in the now – only when I am actually with the thing I perceive.

When my writer is present, I see him. When he's not, I have to turn to a world without images or words.

That world is outside perception. It is immaterial.

Now, Freud's second vision. This came later in his work. It's about a psychic apparatus made up of different systems, defining an inner world that interacts with – but is distinct from – the outer world.

In this view, perception isn't part of the psychic structure. It comes from outside and impacts it.

To put it more simply, and perhaps reconcile both views:

Are we part of nature — or did we somehow fall from the sky?

(I'm joking… maybe.)

Last night I had a dream.

I was in the courtyard of a farm, among the barnyard animals. A dog came over and sat next to me. It was peaceful.

Then, suddenly, a large car came barreling into the courtyard. It pushed me toward the back of the shed. There was no more space — I was cornered. Trapped between the cars that had replaced the old farm equipment.

When I tried to escape, a corridor magically opened in front of me. Outside, a woman kindly pointed toward a hill overlooking the nearby town.

I woke up feeling free.

And I thought: Sometimes, my writer tries to lock me into his way of seeing the world. After all, it's his fingers on the keyboard, shaping this narrative. But why was I trapped at the back of the shed? Am I carrying thoughts that modern minds don't want to hear? Am I a messenger of something unacceptable?

Could direct thought be the voice of nature itself?

And is nature trying to speak to us — as Heraclitus said?

Yes. If you pay attention, nature sends signals — through the lives of animals, trees, stones… through particles, through galaxies.

But maybe its signals are silent — immaterial.

Let's take Heraclitus's word: *Logos*.

My writer told me that it's untranslatable. Some call it the "Word," others "Speech," "Reason," "Law," or even "That which governs the world."

But it also refers to what we encounter — in everyday life.

Here's how Heraclitus begins:

> This Logos is always true, yet men fail to understand it — both before hearing it, and once they have.
>
> Even though everything happens according to this Logos, they do not understand it — words and deeds pass them by, just like dreams.

Other people are no more aware of what they do while awake than they are of what they dreamed.

And again:

> This world, the same for all beings — neither gods nor men created it. It always was, is, and will be — an eternal living fire, kindling and extinguishing in rhythm.

Logic tells us that the world evolves, that time has a past and a future, that species advance, that a human being is the most developed animal...

But maybe the world of sleep offers a different way of seeing. Of thinking. Of being.

My writer told me the sad story of Orpheus and Eurydice.

They marry. But omens loom. Eurydice dies — bitten by a snake.

Orpheus grieves deeply, then dares to descend into the Underworld. He begs Pluto and Proserpina to release Eurydice — not from death itself but only for a while. Out of love.

Moved, they agree. Eurydice can follow him — on one condition: he must not turn around before they reach the world of the living.

Here's how Ovid describes what happened next:

> Through lands of eternal night they walked. Orpheus led, Eurydice followed. The path was steep and narrow. They

were almost home when Orpheus, anxious and longing, turned to see her.

At once, she vanished. A shadow. A breath. He reached for her, but held only air.

For breaking the law of the Underworld, she was lost — forever.

To leave Tartarus, to return to life, we must not look back.

Maybe that's a warning: about what happens when we wake from sleep.

Chapter 18

Dead and Alive at the Same Time

Do some dreams show us glimpses of a second life — of sleep, of Tartarus, of the world of shadows, of death? Yes — because if we are both dead and alive, then we no longer need to burden ourselves with thoughts of an afterlife. We are already there.

Right now, I'm placing my paw on his tablet screen. Yes, I have something to say — because I know a thing or two about sleep.

My writer once told me that about 30 years ago, he lived in the mountains. One night, returning to his chalet, he heard a cry of distress: a cat was stuck at the top of a tall cherry tree outside the house. He climbed the tree and brought the cat down, placing it on his shoulder. That evening, he was with a friend who gave the cat a name inspired by its color. Years later, my writer gave me the same name, because the color on my back matched that cat's.

I don't like this story much. But I know that his friend became attached to that earlier cat — the one who used to perch on his shoulder and lick his nostrils. That cat only stayed for a few days, then vanished, leaving behind a powerful memory. My writer no longer calls me by that name. Still, it saddens me. Why give me the same name? Did he think I was the same cat? That I was both dead and alive?

Yes — because if we are both dead and alive, if we die every night or every day (your choice), then the cessation of biological functions becomes entirely relative. And if we dare push this madness further: are we sure that the one who wakes up in the morning is the same one who went to sleep?

My writer once told me about Pirandello's final play, *I giganti della montagna* (The Mountain Giants). It tells of a villa inhabited by strange beings — dreamlike creatures led by a mysterious master of ceremonies named Cotrone. These beings, the Scalognati ("the Unlucky Ones"), can project their dreams and desires onto the villa's walls, watching them come to life.

One night, a troupe of exhausted actors arrive, led by Ilse, an actress haunted by the suicide of a former lover. In the villa, the actors begin to inhabit bodies not their own. One, still under the villa's influence, hangs himself and becomes the poet who died for Ilse. Panic follows. Cotrone reassures them: each night the villa transforms into music and dreams — and those dreams live outside of us, incoherent and unknown.

The actors, joined by the Unlucky Ones, plan to perform their play before the mountain giants — beings of brute strength who have lost the ability to think. The play ends here, unfinished, with Pirandello's death. Will the actors perform? Will the giants destroy them? We'll never know.

But we do know the play Ilse intended to perform: *The Tale of the Exchanged Child*. A mother, convinced that witches have replaced her child with a monster, fights to reclaim her real, princely son.

Why tell you this? Because it speaks of sleep, of one reality replacing another. Of dual existence.

Yes — but I am the sleep expert, and I ought to tell you more about that other world.

I've said before, I don't need to distinguish between waking and dreaming. I see shadows even when I'm awake. These worlds coexist for me. It's you who divide them.

The first human probably dreamed and thought at the same time. Division came later — when humans began separating everything: idea and its opposite, positive and negative, love and hate, life and death...

Freud, the father of psychoanalysis, did the same: splitting consciousness and unconsciousness, reality and pleasure, instincts and censors, life drives and death drives. Religions also imposed dualities: earthly life versus the afterlife, hell and paradise, reward and punishment. Truth was torn from falsehood; space and time were solidified into rigid constructs; logic began to war with imagination.

And then came the great divide: humans versus all other living beings.

Maybe one day you'll understand: our way of being is just as valid as yours. Speaking and writing doesn't make your ideas superior. Just because you can describe phenomena, formulate hypotheses, or run experiments doesn't mean you own knowledge.

As a cat, I defend a different kind of thought: one without form or language. A thought that's invisible, like the wind. A thought like Heraclitus's river, or the sun — new every day.

And what about Oedipus and his famous riddle?

Everyone focuses on the father's murder and the mother's marriage. Everyone congratulates Oedipus for solving the riddle. Yes, a human being crawls on four legs, walks on two, then leans on a cane.

But riddles are meant to open meaning, not close it off.

Maybe Schrödinger would say that answering the question collapses the possibility — like a quantum wave collapsing into a single state.

The Sphinx throws herself into the abyss, but perhaps Oedipus does too. His arrogance lies in thinking the riddle has only one answer. He ignores what the Sphinx truly offered: three legs, three voices, three possibilities.

He chose only one: to be what was said of him. That he would kill his father and marry his mother.

He could have chosen differently. He could have said, "Both my parents wanted me dead. I must carry the weight of life and death, of being alive and dead at once." But instead, he divided himself. One part accused the other. And he pierced his eyes — just as his feet had once been pierced.

Yes, my writer believes that a riddle poses questions we aren't meant to answer. Maybe that's the difference between humans and cats. For me, everything is always new. A door isn't always a door. My world constantly changes.

For you, it's different. Once you name something, you expect it to stay the same.

But ask someone who fears closed spaces if a door is always a door. Ask someone with a phobia if naming an animal makes the fear disappear.

There are two ways to speak on a psychoanalyst's couch:

One is to speak freely — without purpose, without logic, without memory.

The other is to analyze — to explain, to interpret before feeling.

This morning, my writer admitted that he has never read Erwin Schrödinger's writings — just the anecdote about the cat. But this afternoon, he found a lecture called "Mind and Matter," from 1956. It began:

> We are faced with a remarkable situation. The world we perceive is constructed entirely by our mind via the senses. Yet the conscious mind itself cannot be found within this construct. It has no place. We locate the personality inside the body — but it is not actually there. It has no position in space.

He goes on:

> We think of the personality as being behind the eyes — but it's not.

Reading this gave us chills. It felt like we had already thought these things — without having read them. Once again, we see how thought can transcend time. Schrödinger's mind still speaks.

And that image of the space between the eyes — we had imagined that point, long before reading this text.

Later, Schrödinger adds:

> The eye is the only sensory organ we don't view passively. Naively, we imagine rays projecting from it — rather than light entering it.

And he concludes:

> When facing the body of a deceased loved one, there is comfort in realizing that their true presence was never contained in that body. It was only symbolic.

He quotes Aldous Huxley's *The Perennial Philosophy*:

> There is miraculous agreement among humans of all races and beliefs, separated by millennia, who never knew each other — and yet shared the same fundamental truths.

Maybe Schrödinger's cat — his thought-experiment — carries a meaning that lives on. Maybe that cat, imagined and paradoxical, is more alive than many real ones. For us, he's alive and dead — like all of us.

In fact, maybe he's more alive than dead.

Maybe Schrödinger immortalized him.

Chapter 19

Body … Mind

My friend put on some Native American music — it inspires him too. Yes, this flute, cautiously finding its way through the forest foliage, teaches us that we must advance gently, first feeling what touches all our senses before we quicken our steps. Yes, to feel that each tiny point of this vegetation makes deep contact with every part of our body and mind, and to realize that dividing our being into body and spirit no longer makes sense.

Yes — body and mind intertwine, merge, and become one.

We observe and are observed. Sensations go both ways. We move toward the object, and the object moves toward us. We give up the idea that our gaze takes precedence over its own — that of the object. Yes, the forest looks at me and reaches deep within me. I am part of it. I am it…

The flute continues. Now she calls out — notes shaped like questions, scattered dots, reaching into the treetops, searching for echoes. The sounds grow muffled, as if dialoguing with the subterranean world of the woods. The notes lengthen, like repeated unanswered questions. Finally, the forest replies — with brief, high-pitched notes. Yes, the answer comes from the birds. The flute moves more freely now, able to express itself.

The music becomes continuous, more melodic. Different flutes begin to converse in harmony, questions and answers overlapping in a dialogue that continuously enriches itself — never ending in a full stop…

Last night, my writer had a strange dream. Someone was typing on a keyboard, and months later, their writing was imprinting itself on people's minds, as if it melted into them, leaving no trace. I loved this dream. It reveals a direct transmission of knowledge — like what happens between my writer and me.

And, amusingly, the reverse is true too: my formless thoughts inscribe themselves into his mind, and he manages to translate them into... written traces. An idea comes to us — it makes us dizzy: what if our ancient writers worked like this, as in a dream? What if their writings had already melted into our minds? Then we would carry libraries within ourselves — contrary to that philosopher (whom we've already mentioned) who claimed he would converse with animals only when they had libraries.

Well — we are ready now. We would be happy to converse with him... if he knows how to read what hasn't yet been written.

Would that mean that nature has no fixed forms? That it is like Heraclitus's sun, new every day? Yes — nature would be ever-changing, elusive, undefinable.

But let's return to everyday life.

Right now, my writer isn't at the mill. He's 150 kilometers away, in the city where he works. This evening, he stopped to buy something to cook. The young woman at the checkout looked exhausted, her mind clearly somewhere else. He mentioned it was almost closing time. She asked, "Is it that obvious?" She admitted her mind was already home.

Are we sure our minds are always in the same place as our bodies?

Where are the children we say "have their heads in the clouds"? Yes — their minds are elsewhere. But where exactly? Are they somewhere else, or are they nowhere?

When my writer hears his colleagues speak about the "internal world," he always wonders: where is this internal world? Some neurophysiologists locate it between neurons. Others say we have a soul — some even claim to have weighed it. They say it's between 21 and 45 grams.

Chapter 20

Heraclitus

We've already spoken about the term *logos*. It's a difficult word to translate. Heraclitus tells us:

> Listening not to me but to the Logos, it is wise to acknowledge that all things are one.

Do *logos* and nature meet? Yes:

> To be temperate is the greatest virtue. Wisdom consists in speaking and acting the truth, giving heed to the nature of things.

> Nature loves to hide itself.

> The lord whose oracle is in Delphi neither indicates clearly nor conceals, but gives a sign.

Last night, my writer dreamed of one of his former colleagues – someone who had passed away years ago. He was there, silent, just standing. But something in his presence radiated more intensely than anything else in the scene, as though light itself emanated from him. Let's consider Heraclitus's Fragment 66:

> Immortals become mortals, mortals become immortals; they live in each other's death and die in each other's life.

And Fragment 113:

> It is one and the same thing to be living and dead, awake or asleep, young or old. The former aspect in each case becomes the latter, and the latter becomes the former, by sudden unexpected reversal.

I'll let my writer continue down his somewhat obscure path, but now it's my turn.

It's true that the references he offers to Heraclitus help free us from conventional thinking — but we should also try to bring these ideas into our daily lives. Because, when you look closely, my thinking is not as free as we've claimed. Yes, my thoughts have form. Even if I usually move as though I'm discovering the world anew with every step, I still have points of reference: the rug in front of the door to the living room, the small mat on the terrace against the house, the red-brick column marking the border between the veranda and the forest, the large wooden beam lying at the other end of the terrace.

Why all these details? Because they make up the geography of my everyday life.

Do I also have a sense of time? Yes, my time is shaped by waiting. In the morning, I wait for him to open the French window that leads to my food bowl. If he sleeps in, I nudge his head with mine. Sometimes I nibble his fingers. I also wait for him to sit in our armchair, where I rest on his lap.

He leaves for the workweek soon after. He feels sad when he goes. Even though he tells himself we're still connected at a distance, the separation hurts. As for me, I don't know how to anticipate departure. When he shuts the window shutters, it hits me — I'm face to face with his absence. It's a shock, because I can't imagine the future or reassure myself that he'll return.

So we had to invent something — a way not to lose each other completely.

Have we built an illusion? Can we really keep communicating from afar?

He is certainly connected to me in thought. He can picture me in the familiar places where I tend to be. As for me, since I can't picture him, I return to those spaces linked to his presence: the chair on the terrace where he writes when the sun is out. For me, that chair is him. When he sits in it, it's like he's entering my world. That chair remains even after he disappears. It's my time-traveling chair.

Last night, he had two opposing dreams.

In the first, a half-page of text appeared before his eyes, the letters forming in the air without any visible support. The text began: "The man from Ephesus..." He couldn't read any more than that.

In the second, he was in an old library, the floor a gleaming, polished parquet. Silently, the walls of the library collapsed. Fearing the floor might give way, he and a few others clung to U-shaped iron bars jutting from the one wall still standing.

The first dream echoed one of his ideas — that ancient thought still floats in the air. Ephesus was Heraclitus's home. What appeared wasn't a text by Heraclitus, but about him. After all, the fragments we have today come through the words of others. We possess no full writings from him.

The second dream might be the continuation of the first: even if libraries fall, there will always be someone who remembers.

But what of the U-shaped bars? They resembled steps in a ladder — but they were spaced too far apart to climb. I remind him that he had these dreams while sleeping away from me. Yes, something breaks down when we're apart. He must cling to letters, to writing, to Ephesus...

And he has no proof that we're writing this book together. Sometimes, he believes it's all just in his mind — that I have nothing to do with it.

But he does see me placing my paw on his screen. He does hear me insistently meowing, urging him to sit in our chair.

He has no proof. Only intuition.

He must trust it — and not let himself be discouraged by those who always translate everything into egocentric terms. He is not alone.

I am here.

And I believe... I love him.

Yes, we love each other. And through that love, we are able to write.

Chapter 21

The State of Mind

My writer dreamed of a six-holed Native American flute. He tried to play the highest notes by closing the lowest holes. Of course, he didn't need to close all of them – he could, for instance, have left the third hole open. Technically, that makes sense. But we're going to approach this dream a little differently.

My writer has often thought that psychoanalysis tends to look downward – into the patient's past, toward early experiences. It sometimes forgets to look upward – toward the higher notes, the ones that belong to thought. When you talk about internal objects, unconscious fantasies, imagos – do you really believe all of that is inside you? These may be useful concepts in psychoanalytic practice, but they're human theories. None of it really sparks my curiosity.

What does interest me are the words "state of mind."

Let's start with the word "spirit." For me, spirit simply *is*. It leaves no trace, has no past or future, defies categorization. It's immaterial – like wind, like thought, like love.

So then, what is a state of mind?

As the phrase suggests, it's the condition in which the spirit finds itself. Think of Schrödinger's cat: when you open the box to see if it's dead or alive, the spirit condenses, precipitates, into form. The philosopher Edmund Husserl might have said that the spirit presents itself within us.

Yes, for us, spirit is everywhere. It isn't bound by space or time – it's in everything: living, created, desired, or even composed of particles or black photons.

Whew. My writer's mind tends to drift into abstraction. He enjoys sailing toward the farthest reaches of the conceptual. Thankfully, I keep my paws planted on solid ground.

To him, the mind is an ultimate abstraction. But for me, it's part of everyday life — something I can sense directly, as if I had my nose right up against it. I see it like a texture in space and time, a probabilistic cloud shifting between light and shadow, visible and invisible.

Maybe we've both gone a little mad — his madness being the idea that the mind is one, like in the Upanishads: I am Brahman — absolute reality — One and Many. Time is my Shakti, negating the self... And mine? It's believing that state of mind is the individual translation of a mind without measure — a reading of Heraclitus's *logos*.

Our madnesses meet — briefly uniting the obscure wisdom of the pre-Socratics with the spirit of the Vedas. *Veda*, in ancient Indian and Sanskrit, means "vision" or "knowledge." It's a collection of texts said to have been revealed to sages known as rishis.

Last night it was my turn to dream. It wasn't quite a dream — more of an animated vision. A band scrolled horizontally. At either end, an arrow rose vertically. All together it formed a "U" — like in one of my writer's previous dreams.

The horizontal band was unreadable, like a text searching for its shape — just as I imagine writing. One arrow gave a sense of unity; the other radiated chaos. Perhaps those arrows represent our coming together and our drifting apart. The scrolling band, then, would symbolize the weave between our states of mind.

Yes, because even though spirit — *logos* — is common to all, each individual state of mind connects with or separates from others. Together, these form a cloud of light points and shadow points.

Let's try to organize this:

- *Logos*: the shared current of spirit (the horizontal band);
- Two forces: one unifying, one dividing (the vertical vectors).

Freud might call these the life and death drives — one binding, the other disintegrating, returning us to the inanimate.

Empedocles already knew this:

> I shall tell thee a twofold tale. At one time it grew to be one only out of many; at another, it divided up to be many instead of one ...

I believe spirit is One, common to all. Each of us — those with spirit (yes, I'm teasing) — draws from that One to shape our own state of mind. It's a way of thinking that removes the line between material and immaterial — and frees us from the idea that the soul is locked inside the body.

Last night, I had another vision.

The flute returned, but this time it only had three holes. Strangely, when I focused deeply, a fourth hole formed — as if the wood hollowed itself from within, like the sand in an hourglass forming a small crater.

The other day, my writer played his Navajo flute for the first time while I sat on his lap. I looked around, trying to find where the sound was coming from. For me, it wasn't coming from the flute — it filled the whole space. That tells you something: what I perceive isn't always localized. When I hunt, I can focus with laser precision, but most of the time, my perception is diffuse.

It's as if I feel everything all at once, and only later do I focus on a single point. My gaze narrows only after the world washes over me in a kind of sensory cloud.

And that makes me wonder:

Is our communication — yours and mine — happening through that diffuse cloud?

Or is it point to point?

Chapter 22

We Are Two

Last night, it was my writer's turn to dream. He was driving along a circular road; the road sloped gently, white, maybe snowy. It felt as though he were driving on Jupiter's ring. He woke up thinking it was time to leave behind the story of the cat who is both dead and alive. I agree.

Besides, this book must be able to distinguish itself from what physicists or ancient thinkers have said. It was the previous owners of the mill who gave me my first name. They called me Boulledeneige, Snowball. My writer never quite understood why there were two Ls — until this morning. He realized that *boulle* meant both "ball" and "bubble." Perhaps the former owners had a dog in mind, and a young boy from a famous comic strip. But my writer imagined the difference between a ball and a bubble — one solid, the other fragile and transparent.

But why did he recall my old name just after dreaming of a snowy road — or Jupiter's gaseous ring?

What matters is that I've reclaimed my original name. I no longer want to carry someone else's. I've found my own name again. I no longer want to be the shadow of the dead.

We're clearly at a turning point in our writing. Maybe now I can express myself more freely, and maybe my writer can finally let go of the crown of... Zeus, and come back down to earth — to our present, not only to the world of ancient thought.

This morning, I was there, on the small table at the house entrance, just as I always am when he arrives. As always, he kissed my forehead before feeding me. Then, after breakfast, I did my usual loop around the house and reappeared on the terrace, where he served my second plate. This is our ritual.

He stayed with me on the terrace for a while before going inside to light the stove, turn on the radiators, and prepare his meal. Meanwhile, I wandered in and out, meowing until he settled into his armchair — so I could curl up on his lap.

Now that I'm no longer living in someone else's name, and he's no longer trying to align our experiences with the "oneness" of ancient philosophy, our relationship is evolving. He has to think of me without imposing his way of thinking on mine.

Our journey has explored ideas from particle physics, pre-Socratic philosophers, Greek mythology, and Native American wisdom. It's helped us stage our own Copernican revolution — to dethrone humanity from the imaginary center of the universe, from the illusion of being its sole observer.

So now... what will we talk about?

After all this, my writer dreamed again — this time of being in Africa with a friend. Each had a different destination but only one car between them, making travel plans difficult. Maybe that reflects where we are now: until recently, my writer believed he was merely translating my thoughts. But now he sees that the literary references have always been his. In truth, he had been using me to make his points. Now, there really are two of us. Our thoughts must now move side by side, no longer filtered through just one voice.

And why Africa? Perhaps a nod to colonization or missionary conquest. Until now, I was his Man Friday — his wild companion, taught to think like a civilized person. But no — I can't think like a human. And he can't think like a cat.

So we must invent a new geometry, and start from zero.

Right now, I'm grooming myself, then drifting off to sleep. My writer wonders whether this state of mine is precisely an absence of thought. He'd call it a pure existential state. And when I emerge from that state, I explore — mainly to verify that my world remains unchanged.

Lately, even small noises make me flee. Sometimes I run away when there's no noise at all. There's a large yellow object in the bathroom — a pressure washer. It frightens me. But this morning, I mustered the courage to crawl toward it. I studied it thoroughly, especially the long black hose extending from its yellow body. I rubbed my cheeks against it, nudged it with my nose, as if to test its force with my own skin.

Today the weather is wild. It's raining hard. I took shelter in the oldest part of the mill. It's true — I can't always live in reference to him. I need solitude, even when we're together. Sometimes we must separate, if only to make separations easier to bear. Like a homeopathic dose of absence — an echo of absence. After having lived so closely, having written so many pages together, it's time we each think from within our own worlds.

If our states of mind were always aligned, we might lose the sense of being someone. His mind is always at work, generating ideas. Mine is mostly silent. In this sense, we complete each other: he struggles to find peace; I live mostly in serenity.

And yet, when he's inside, I still meow until he sits down — because if he doesn't, I grow anxious and wander aimlessly. But now the rain has quieted, and I've returned to him. Before settling beside him, I did what he calls my *tour du propriétaire*: I climbed up one of his arms, over his shoulder, across the back of the chair, and down the other side — like a feline amusement-park ride.

Today, we realize that we must guess what the other is thinking. Maybe humans face the same challenge. You think your words reveal your thoughts — but do they, truly?

In the end, my writer and I may never fully know what the other experiences. But we share profound moments of intimacy. And we each experience those moments in our own way. What matters is not whether we see the same thing but that we meet somewhere.

You humans think you're in the same world – but a gulf separates you. And language often fails to bridge it.

For me, it's all unspoken. A silent being. My writer refers here to Heidegger. But even Heidegger, for all his thinking, cannot grasp the simplicity of just being. For my writer, the idea of being stirs unease. And let's not be too hard on him – he does still have to write something legible.

For me, being is being. For my writer, he must think in order to be. A certain philosopher said that already.

Let's go back to the terrace. When he sits on one of the stone benches around the round stone table, I sit beside him. I move behind him. I return beside him. Sometimes, he sits on the grass, and I place myself a meter away. Then I become still. Time stops. Space vanishes. A virtual point of contact emerges.

Is it an illusion? A vision? A kind of sacred delirium?

Speaking of furrows and plows – not everything in your world has been plowed. Not all growth begins with seeds. And not everything that grows was ever planted.

This is where our ways of seeing diverge – and converge. You divide time into past, present, and future. You say the past no longer exists, and the future does not yet exist. But that's only because you've divided time.

You divide space too. You speak of here and elsewhere. But I'm always here, always now. Of course, I sometimes meow to go outside – but that only means my here feels incomplete. I always return to my now.

It's like I'm flipping the page of a book that has only one page.

No matter how many times I turn it, I land back on the same one.

You say cats always land on their feet. Maybe this is why.

Sometimes the page is clear, like when he crouches down and I run to him. Sometimes, it's blurred – like the other day when he reached out to help me down from a tree, and my paw twitched away. In that moment, he wasn't on my page.

Yes, my page changes — but remains the same.

He, on the other hand, knows the difference between being at the mill and being in the city. But he carries me in another way — in his thoughts, in his heart. I live deep inside him. It doesn't depend on what he thinks — I'm already there.

And he lives deep in me, too.

I believe that what happened between classical physics and quantum physics is happening between individuals, too.

We exist on two levels.

On one, we are separate.

On the other, that whole construct dissolves — into entanglement, superposition, probability. Beyond this threshold, there is no more identity, no more causality, no more separation. Beyond this limit lies the unknown. The unknowable. The invisible, silent link between us.

My writer says this silent connection exists in psychoanalysis too, when something unspoken passes between people. I tell him — for me, that's the only way I communicate.

He leads group therapy and wonders whether it's the silent participants who carry the group's deepest truth.

It's hard for humans not to speak. Maybe that's why we started writing — to make my silence coexist with his words.

But when you read, do you really read only the words?

Don't you read between the lines?

Poets would agree.

Why are we drawn to pre-Socratic philosophy?

Because Socrates marked the shift to a human-centered world. He was condemned, accused of not honoring the gods.

Let's recall:

MELITUS: "I accuse you of recognizing no god."

SOCRATES: "What? I don't believe, like other men, that the sun and moon are gods?"

> MELITUS: "No, by Jupiter – he says the sun is a stone, and the moon an earth!"

Socrates tried to free wisdom from divine authority. He placed understanding above mystery.

He also said:

> The poet is not guided by reason, but by natural inspiration – like prophets or seers who speak great truths but understand nothing of what they say.

Understanding, for Socrates, was the path to wisdom.

But perhaps, like Oedipus, he was wrong to try to understand the enigma.

Maybe the language of the gods was never meant to be deciphered.

Can humans claim to possess their own fire, or must they accept that it's only a reflection of something greater?

You know the myth of Narcissus.

His mirror is like mine – unreflective.

But unlike him, I don't fall in love with my image. I cherish the gaze of my writer. He sees me. I see him. No glass between us. We are one, in the middle.

And when we are apart, we still see each other, through a kind of second sight.

An inner eye. A heart's hallucination.

A mirror, infinite, unbroken.

Chapter 23

Unbeknownst to Us

Last night, I had a vision. A human head was emerging from a horse's mouth. The rest of the human's body was still inside the horse, and to make this possible, they had opened the animal's flank. The result was a horse with a human head — the long equine muzzle replaced by a round, hairless head, without a mane.

My writer once told me that in English, the phrase "straight from the horse's mouth" means you are absolutely certain of what you're saying. In English, there's also "let the cat out of the bag" — to reveal a secret. In French, they say: *à cheval donné on ne regarde pas la bouche* — "never look a gift horse in the mouth." One should be happy with a gift, even if it has a flaw.

Of course, my favorite idiom is the one about letting the cat out of the bag — or even better — out of the box. Yes, it's high time I escaped from the box Erwin Schrödinger imagined locking me in. I no longer want to be both dead and alive. I want to be alive — and certain of what I'm saying.

I'm convinced that the way we cats communicate exists within every human being. It's your most essential way of being — so deeply ingrained that it goes unnoticed, like breathing. So present, so self-evident, that it can't even be thought about.

As we've said, the founder of psychoanalysis used the term *unbewusst* — "without knowing," "involuntarily," "automatically." It's been translated as "unconscious," but that translation may have stripped the word of its richness. Freud's method of free association — asking the patient to speak freely, without judgment or censorship — was a technique meant to guide the mind toward the unknown. But in theory, Freud tried to dress up the unknown, filling it with representations and affects. In other words, he wanted to open the box of mystery — but then label everything inside.

He believed dreams led toward the unknown, but perhaps he rushed to define their meaning — limiting them to "daytime residues," sensory experiences, and sexuality. Since when has the unknown been confined to sex?

Yes, children's curiosity focuses on sexuality, but Freud may have confused childhood curiosity with human curiosity. From the beginning of time, humans have been drawn to the unknown — the stars, the void, mystery, the sacred, the beyond. What transcends, what escapes comprehension.

In wanting to reveal the unknown, Freud ultimately trapped humanity inside its own psychic apparatus. He reduced all mystical experience — the mystery of life and death — to childhood fantasies and instincts. Even the oceanic feeling, that boundless sense of unity, became nothing more than wishful illusion.

I think my writer was inspired by the image of the horse with the human head. It allowed him to speak — literally — from the horse's mouth, and finally let me, the cat, out of the box. Psychoanalysis is his profession, and he still believes in the power of free association. But even he admits that sometimes theory becomes liturgy, and liturgy becomes dogma.

So I'll step in now, to bring psychoanalysis back down to earth, to make it accessible — even to the nearest stray cat.

If we cats had invented a science, it would be the science of presence. A science of being there, not of representing the world. We've observed the world our way for millennia. We still chase strings as if they were living creatures. But what does it mean to be alive?

Have humans, in defining their identity, stepped away from life itself?

We cats haven't followed this path of separation. We live without naming it. We exist without declaring it.

So I ask: Can we be alive and know we are alive? Can we exist and be aware of it?

Does a tree, a stone, or a cell know it is alive?

When people lose their memory, they become, in a way, like us. Timeless. Outside of past and future. Present without knowing it.

But then — why work so hard to help them recover memory?

Couldn't they be showing us a different way to live? A life outside your social codes and definitions of selfhood?

Why obsess over the damaged brain and ignore the possibility of another kind of awareness?

You see, I understand these people. I sometimes don't recognize my writer when I see him outside our familiar spaces. It's strange — we are one from a distance, yet don't recognize each other when we're face to face.

Yes, it's paradoxical, but only if you insist on using one kind of logic.

Let me explain another way. My writer once told me about a man who visited his elderly mother every Thursday. They would lunch at the same restaurant. Yet the mother addressed her son using her late husband's name — and spoke of "her son," meaning the man right in front of her.

Another mother, in the presence of her two daughters, would speak to one of them about "the one who calls me every day" — again, speaking of the daughter sitting right there.

How can you explain this? I feel it too, when I see my writer in the barn. We are connected from a distance but don't always recognize each other in proximity. Those two mothers aren't just confused — they're in contact with another layer of reality. Perhaps they've lost touch with what you call reality but have gained access to something else.

After all, "demented" just means "without reason."

Have they lost their minds, or have they found another one?

As a cat, I'm also "without reason" — but I don't feel mindless.

My writer often says that René Descartes wasn't as Cartesian as people believe. Listen to what Descartes wrote:

> I suppose, accordingly, that all the things which I see are false ... that none of those objects which my fallacious memory represents ever existed ... I believe that body, figure, extension, motion, and place are merely fictions of my mind. What is there, then, that can be esteemed true? Perhaps only this: that there is absolutely nothing certain.

And then:

> It must be maintained ... that this proposition, I am, I exist, is necessarily true every time I pronounce it, or conceive it in my mind.

And further:

> I have frequently, during sleep, believed that I perceived objects which I afterward observed I did not in reality perceive.

I love these lines.

They reflect how we cats think. Nothing is certain. And yet, every time I say "I exist," I do exist — at least for that moment. In saying it, I define myself, separating from Heraclitus's flowing *logos* to affirm my individual being.

But — if I carry within me the idea of an infinite substance, mustn't it come from something infinite?

My writer has gone deep again, into the forest of thought. Let me pull us back.

By saying "I exist," humans have come to see themselves as individuals.

But I have never said it.

I have never claimed to be anything at all.

I exist without knowing it, without needing to affirm it.

I have no need to divide or categorize.

I've never felt the urge to dissect, to *analyze* — to untie, as the root of the word suggests.

Chapter 24

Everything Is Number

Last night, my writer dreamed of a device that would allow my teleportation. But the operation was incomplete. What arrived at the destination wasn't my body — it was only an unfinished mathematical formula. Eventually, he managed to complete the equation, which then became directly connected to me. What had been teleported was not my physical form but rather an abstraction — a synthesis, like a mathematical blueprint of my living essence, a kind of genetic sequence.

This dream gave us a lot to think about. My writer recalled the work of American anesthesiologist Stuart Hameroff, who studied microtubules — microscopic structures inside certain cells, especially neurons. For him, these microstructures might contain something like a digital memory, a computerization of our being. And it is through this mysterious encoding that he explores... reincarnation.

But for me, this dream has nothing to do with the transmigration of souls. In his dream, my writer tries to teleport me — not as a body but as a formula. I do not appear in flesh and fur but as a mathematical sequence, initially incomplete, eventually resolved. That's when I thought of Pythagoras, who said: "Everything is number."

Number is the unique principle of the world; it is the uncreated, autogenous force, stretched like a chain across the world. It produces being, sustains life, and ensures the permanence of individuals, of species, of the whole. All that is is through the One — and is one. The One is immanent in things, since it constitutes their essence; but at the same time, it is transcendent, since it belongs to all and is exhausted by none. This One — endowed with life and movement — contains within it reason, *logos*, unfolding in harmony and measured by number, acquiring in this process the perfection it lacks.

When I hear Pythagoras speak, it's as if I hear music – poetic harmony. It resonates with me, even though I don't speak in words. Pythagoras's reason doesn't reason – it resonates. Perhaps that's the difference between cats and humans: humans reason, while nature resonates within us.

I also love this image of number as an uncreated force, a golden thread stretched across the world. My writer often marvels at the harmony in my movements – how I leap, land, climb, and navigate without effort. When I walk across the round kitchen table, winding through its many obstacles, I never knock anything over. I have four legs, and yet I dance like a number in motion.

When I climb the ladder leading to the living-room beams, I do so with elegance and precision. Watching me, my writer once thought: This is number in motion. Not calculation but harmony. In Pythagoras, number is not something we compute – it is the very pattern of life.

Pythagorean music, for example, was built on arithmetic. It imposed rules on instruments and voices – and rejected mere sensory pleasure as unworthy of true harmony. The Pythagorean musical scale used thirds and quarter-tones, which modern ears might find strange – but some say they resemble the meowing of cats. Which suggests, perhaps playfully, that our sounds are closer to the harmony of numbers than to the harmony pleasing to human ears. Another clue, if needed, that we cats are children of antiquity.

Consider the famous Pythagorean theorem. In a right-angled triangle, the square of the hypotenuse equals the sum of the squares of the other two sides. If the sides measure 3 and 4, then $3^2 + 4^2 = 9 + 16 = 25$. The hypotenuse is 5. That's a number you can count, measure, visualize.

But if the two sides each measure 1, the sum of their squares is 2, and the hypotenuse is $\sqrt{2}$ – an irrational number. In Latin, *ratio* means "to count." An irrational number, then, is a number that cannot be counted – because it contains an infinite number of non-repeating decimals. A number that never ends. A number that escapes.

So, from a simple triangle, we are launched into two different worlds. One is measurable. The other – immeasurable. Even if we can draw the triangle on a page, the number that describes its hypotenuse is beyond measure. Perhaps it belongs to another dimension.

This triangle, then, stands with two feet on the ground, grounded in measurable reality – and a third that stretches toward something else. Something incalculable.

Chapter 25

The Oedipal Triangle

Yes, certainly, the child must triangulate between love for his mother and rivalry with his father, or vice versa. However, Oedipus, by killing his father and marrying his mother, collapses the triangle, which is thus reduced to a straight line that leads to his own destruction. Jocasta tries to show him another path — one of fantasy, one of dreams: Do not fear uniting with your mother, for in their dreams, many men have dreamed of doing so. Oedipus wants the truth to come to light. And the truth is that his mother willed her own death:

> OEDIPUS: What! she, she gave it thee?
> HERDSMAN: 'Tis so, my king.
> OEDIPUS: With what intent?
> HERDSMAN: To make away with it.
> OEDIPUS: What, she its mother.
> HERDSMAN: Fearing a dread weird.
> OEDIPUS: What weird?
> HERDSMAN: 'Twas told that he should slay his ...

At this point, there's no longer any talk of marrying his mother; it's only about the murder of his parents. But then, what had the oracle actually predicted?

Now he's off into triangles and theorems. I don't know what he wants to prove. Yes, I couldn't take it when he embarked on his solitary crusade, and I pointed it out by stroking his face with my paw. Because when he throws himself into his supposed knowledge, he doesn't always take into account what I might be thinking inside my little cat head. Yes, he can quote Sophocles, the riddle of the Sphinx, and talk about the Pythagorean theorem, irrational numbers, or a diagonal in a dimension without measure. This is certainly because he sometimes talks about our way of thinking with colleagues who reject our worldview. Yes, sometimes he sparks hostile — sometimes even violent — reactions from those who cling to strictly rational thought, who follow the creed of cause and effect, who defend the strict historicity of events, who think everything must be proven experimentally and that knowledge must only be transmitted through academia...

Faced with these conflicting discussions, he tends to argue, and these debates spill over into our writing. He could let go of his Don Quixote role and stop casting me as his servant, Sancho Panza, to find a more modest role, closer to companionship with me. Because when he's showing off his knowledge, he sometimes prevents me from expressing my point of view.

Where we do agree is on the idea that beneath intellect, emotion, and even the sensory, there's another kind of sensitivity — direct, silent, hard to define with words. It's said that whales, in addition to emitting sounds that travel long distances, whisper to their young at short range — within about a hundred meters. Rubbing myself against him is my way of whispering... that I'm here with him, that I'm attached to him, that I'm maintaining contact.

We might even say that when union and separation breathe together, a kind of balance is reached — whereas if one dominates, the risk of rupture is greater. And that might free us from the idea of the cat being both dead and alive, and instead allow us to say: the cat's life and death are part of a kind of pulse, where life and death alternate like the beat of a heart — systole, when the heart contracts, and diastole, when it relaxes — or like the rhythm of breath: inhale, exhale...

Last night, my writer dreamed of a word engraved on a stone. The word was made by joining two others, and it was only by covering the top half of this double word that it became legible: aleph. In the dream, it was the first letter of the Egyptian alphabet. My writer is not a linguist, and he wonders where this dream came from. Yes, he had already heard of this word, which is also the first letter of the Hebrew alphabet. Maybe he's thinking of the book in which Freud claims that Moses was Egyptian. But why this word in his dream? That's a mystery. Is the dream telling him to return to the first letter, to go back to the beginning, to trace the birth of writing?

Here's a slightly wild idea — for once — from me: maybe at night we gain access to a kind of knowledge. Easy to say. Always this notion that knowledge isn't just locked away in libraries but that it's also freely accessible… while we sleep.

The dream paused our writing…

Would we wait for the next night to see what came next?

Here's the dream from last night. It was a geometric dream. My writer had to measure the height of a pyramid. To do this, he had to double the length of each side of the square base, and it was this change that made it possible to measure the pyramid's height. Let's take a pyramid with a square base whose faces are equilateral triangles. Without getting into the details of his calculations, my writer found that by doubling the side length of the base, the height of the new pyramid would be four times that of the original. Several ways lead to this conclusion. One is to use the Pythagorean theorem. But more intuitively, we can say that by doubling the length of one side of the base, we get four bases, each the size of the original. Could we have guessed that the new height would be four times as large? It doesn't really matter.

What I like about this pyramid story is that by doubling the base, the height quadruples. When you combine the two dreams, you might think that we have to expand our base, our aleph, to elevate our pyramid even higher. What's interesting here is that these dreams raise questions about knowledge — one about writing, the other about geometry.

So, could dreams be a kind of book that writes itself as it writes? Another way of knowing?

Chapter 26

What About the Brain?

You're used to thinking that consciousness is located in your brain or, as Freud said, in your soul apparatus – in your psyche. We've already seen that my writer prefers the term "state of mind" to "psychic apparatus." Yes, because speaking of a state of mind doesn't necessarily imply that it takes place in a system within us. There wouldn't necessarily be a separation between an internal world and an external one, but rather a breathing space between the state of mind and the spirit of place, and between the state of mind and the spirit of time. Could it be the same for our brain? Could it be a kind of receiver that translates everything that presents itself to it – what's in the air?

The word "spirit" comes from the Latin word for breath, or wind. Yes, we like to think – like Pim van Lommel, a Dutch researcher who worked on near-death experiences – that the brain is a kind of transmitter-receiver:

> When we talk about the brain and consciousness, in my opinion, the brain doesn't produce consciousness. The brain is a facilitator; it makes the experience of consciousness possible. The brain, but also the body, are transmitters-receivers. Compare that with a computer. You can receive more than a billion websites, but these aren't produced by your computer. To receive consciousness, we need our body. Your brain is the instrument, but it doesn't produce consciousness. It only transmits it. Consciousness isn't localized in the brain; it has a non-local aspect – that is, outside of space and time.

My writer likes to compare the function of the brain to the function of dreams. Dreams are said to visualize the experience of sleep — that unknown and unknowable dimension we access while asleep. The brain, like dreams, translates into images what it perceives or receives from this unknowable reality, this unknown that humans have often tried to shape in one way or another. Yes, your brain shapes this unknowable reality by creating a kind of sensory software that shows it a clear and recognizable world.

An American physicist, Leonard Mlodinow, reminds us that what we perceive is actually an interpretation our brain makes based on data collected from our five senses. For example, the text you are reading now is very different from what your brain receives from your eyes.

But our eyes don't see everything, and reality remains partly unknown to us. Still, without going so far as to say that this unknowable reality resembles the terrible truth of *The Matrix*, we could imagine that this other dimension might be accessible to us outside our dreams and outside our brains — yes, directly, instantly, beyond our sensations and emotions.

With me, my writer learns to trust what presents itself to his mind, and with him I learn that I can share thoughts with him — thoughts that are still in search of a thinker, as Wilfred Bion, the English psychoanalyst, once said. Yes, thoughts that do not yet have a form, and maybe never will.

Perhaps enigmas are not meant to be solved! Look at Oedipus, who thought he had solved the riddle of the Sphinx: he had to tear out his eyes so he would no longer see.

Does that mean we must also renounce sight, renounce the reality that our software presents to us? Yes and no. Yes, because this logic was constructed by humans, and their brains help sustain it. No, because this program is necessary to prevent them from being completely overwhelmed by the unknowable.

Did my writer tell you that, when he was in a village in Mauritania, everyone saw the devil – except him? And that those who didn't see the devil risked being possessed by him? The villagers pointed out a little girl who they said was possessed, chained up… her mother didn't see the devil either, and so she couldn't protect her.

Do you really believe that humans from centuries or millennia ago saw the same reality you see now? Like cats – and of course many animals – they could surely visually locate an object. But maybe they also had a kind of floating vision, an eye in waiting, an eye that doesn't see, an eye that – paradoxically – could sense what's invisible to the human eye.

Yes, we cannot see everything – sorry… have everything.

Chapter 27

Reality and Imagination

My writer had to leave early this weekend because he had a class with students. When he closed the shutter on the French window, I moved away and hid behind one of the columns that frame the terrace. These moments of separation are painful. I feel like his departure completely disrupts my vision of the world. Of course, when he leaves, I return to my cat-like habits, in direct contact with the little forest, with the other cats prowling around the mill looking for food, but also with the winter cold and the leafless trees. What I miss is the warm contact with him, the fire in the living-room stove, and my cozy little corner next to his antique bed — my little home within the house.

I sensed that he was sad to leave me so soon, and that he had in mind the speech he was supposed to give to the students. I know that for two days he couldn't write anything. Yes, because in order for him to write, he must not read the writings of other authors; his mind must remain free. Two books somewhat disrupted our inspiration. The first — by Michel Juffé — imagines a correspondence between Freud and Spinoza, a great seventeenth-century Dutch philosopher. What saddened my writer was seeing how Benedictus Spinoza's open-mindedness contrasted with Sigmund Freud's confinement within his rigid conception of the world. The second book was a work by Martin Heidegger about two *pre-Socratic* philosophers — my writer hates that term — Anaximander and Parmenides.

I don't know if Freud had a cat, but he's said to have remarked about us: "Cats, women, and great criminals have this in common: they represent an unattainable ideal and a capacity for self-love that makes them attractive to us."

As I am both a girl and a cat, I feel doubly implicated. Was he blind to our dual capacity to love? Yes, you have to be blind to think that we love only ourselves and that we represent an unattainable ideal. Of course, we go about our business, we have our own lives, but is that enough to label us narcissistic? I would point out that people full of themselves like to look in mirrors, while I don't even recognize myself in them — and sometimes I run away from them.

If Freud really spoke of women as an unattainable ideal, how could he love them? We have loved humans since the dawn of time, and our love is complete; we don't need to divide it into categories like self-love and object-love — meaning love for someone other than ourselves. And when I smooth my fur, it's not out of vanity; I do it in harmony with nature. And when a woman makes herself beautiful, is it for herself? To attract men? Or is she paying homage to aesthetic pleasure, to beauty, to Aphrodite?

Love, for us, is like a fire that animates body, heart, and mind — all without separating them into categories — a fire that flares and fades, like a pulse. And when we move away, the fire turns to smoke, carried by the wind. Then the wind dies down, and it is the air that reunites us.

In the same way, we might think that myths continue to shape us — not because they are ingrained in our psyche as universal structures but because they remain present, still raising their questions and enigmas. The myth remains, whether or not it's crossed the ages.

If Erwin Schrödinger taught us that opening the box collapses a phenomenon that was previously undefined, could it be that Freud tried to drag the gods of Olympus into the depths of the unconscious? And not only the gods — mythical figures like Narcissus, Oedipus, and Prometheus are summoned too. By translating myth into psyche, Freud may have clipped the wings of what myth can offer in a more direct way — without requiring us to assign it meaning or a single interpretation.

Yes, Freud thought he had solved the riddle of the Sphinx. And yes, we love endlessly interpreting that riddle. And if I wanted to play along and solve it, I would say this: my four paws meet the two feet of my writer so that we may discover an idea that transcends our respective thoughts. We believe that beyond or beneath the individual mind, there is the One — whether you call it the Great Mind, the Holy Mind, nature, *logos*, cosmos, the world, the unknown, or the infinite... the choice is yours.

Of course, my writer tries to translate my philosophical thought into words. But my philosophy doesn't consist of making speeches. Maybe my philosophy consists of living outside the passage of time.

Now I'm sitting on his left thigh. I look straight ahead, my eyes half-closed. He looks at me, and I close my eyes, my head slightly bowed. My thoughts seem suspended, so abstract that all sensation disappears. Now I rest my head against his hand. I purr... then even the purring becomes silent... then it returns... I'm transported into the air... toward infinity... colors appear. It's like a long... the sea is bright yellow and the sand purple, almost pink. Yet it feels as though this figure is rising, as if being lifted up, and as it rises, the colors of the beach fade, dissolving into a kind of transparency.

Now I open my eyes. I lick my face with the help of my paw, then climb off his thigh and walk out toward the small forest.

The night was peaceful. I slept on my comfortable cushion, but this morning a strong wind picked up. I hate staying inside when I hear the whistling, creaking, and groaning that the wind makes in our old mill. I meowed for him to open the main door, and I settled down on the little rug outside, preferring to be in direct contact with the force of the wind rather than hear its complaints and laments from within. Maybe it's from the moment we try to shelter ourselves from the forces of nature that we begin to fear them. I'd rather face them than imagine what they're doing — an imagination which, admittedly, I lack.

Humans, on the other hand, by seeking and creating shelter, began to imagine what was happening outside, to represent nature, and eventually to try to study it. So, while I'm directly confronted by what frightens me, my writer must also confront what he imagines. Yes, humans are anxious, and their anxiety goes hand in hand with what they imagine, what they think. That's the price of stepping out of the present – of imagining a past and projecting into a future.

I'm still sitting on my little rug, while he's starting to worry because the storm has caused a power outage, and he's been using candles for the past few hours. But living in the present isn't always easy either – what frightens us still haunts us. For example, the storm has calmed a bit, but I continue to avoid the house, as if the danger were still there. So it's also a disadvantage not to imagine what's happening and not to be able to tell myself that the noises the wind makes in the house will stop once the storm ends. Being stuck in the present can be unsettling too, and I understand why humans are so attached to cause and effect. It gives them a sense of peace.

I'm still outside trying to calm myself, but without success. I wag my tail from side to side. That's what I do when I feel threatened. Outside, I face the elements; that's my way of keeping them in check. Inside, I no longer control the situation. And that... is anxiety.

Chapter 28

Is the World Divisible?

Last night, my writer had a dream that was both precise and strange. A calculation, 7 × 8, kept repeating itself in his mind. He had to divide the number 90 by 8. He didn't think the result would have two digits, and he persisted in using 7 as the answer — realizing that multiplying this number by 8 resulted in a number too small compared to the denominator. It was as if he couldn't imagine a result with multiple digits, as if he were stuck on 7.

Why such a dream? Could this impossible calculation be an expression of difficulty accepting the rigor of arithmetic? Did the dreamer's insistence on repeating the same operation reveal how humans sometimes cling to a way of thinking that turns out to be inadequate? One could speculate endlessly — for example, that the dreamer can't stand decimals, or that he doesn't want to dissociate the 9 from the 0 to divide 90 by 8. Despite all explanations, the dream remains mysterious.

My world is not divisible. It is not calculable, and I do not measure my affection. At most, I can distinguish between +1 and -1, since my way of being is divided between attraction and aversion, between loving and fleeing. I am drawn to nature — or I flee from it. I'm sensitive to what it emits: I approach it if I feel in harmony with it, or I retreat if I sense danger.

Perhaps the first humans experienced nature this way. Then came the desire to understand it, discover its laws, calculate, prove, and reason. But this conquest involved a kind of rupture, a challenge, a power struggle. Put simply: human beings competed with nature to escape terror — the terror of submitting to its unknown and unknowable laws. They sought to possess it, conquer it, colonize it, so they could forget that they themselves were part of a world that surpassed them on every side.

Forget, just for a moment, what you think you've discovered about the laws of nature. For us, nature is one. We don't differentiate between human, animal, plant, mineral... we don't divide body from spirit... we don't need to separate the physical from the metaphysical, the material from the spiritual, the natural from the supernatural. That doesn't mean we believe this One is purely good or immutable.

I think back to the points of light I sometimes perceive above the foreheads of certain humans — and to the shadows that sometimes disturb the atmosphere of the living room. The light concentrates; the shadows fragment and dissolve the space's unity. There's a kind of breath between convergence and diffusion, compactness and dispersion. The eye behaves similarly: it can focus sharply or take in a diffuse impression.

Could the breathing of nature mirror our own? When we inhale, we concentrate the air within us; when we exhale, we release it. And beyond breath as physiology, we could also think of inspiration — as in a sudden insight — and expiration, as in the exhaling of life itself. Inspiration and expiration: union and diffusion, concentration and dissolution.

So, if Descartes sought to demonstrate the existence of God from the idea that humans have of Him, perhaps we demonstrate the existence of the One through humans themselves. For us — as for some philosophers like Heraclitus, Spinoza, and others — all living beings are part of the One, of the *logos*... or, as the Native Americans might say, the Great Spirit. We are united and dissolved in the One, drawn toward the light and shadowed by the dark, inspired and expired, alive and dead...

This morning, my writer told me that after breakfast on the terrace, I fell asleep. As I slept, I let out little meows, unlike those I utter when awake: they were like songs, a kind of composition where wonder, sighs, joy, and anxiety followed one another.

A litany, interrupted now and then by quick breathing and rhythmic murmurs — a mix of fear and delight.

My writer wondered what journey I was on. Could my cushion be a kind of spaceship — not one that travels through galaxies but through the space of sleep? Yes, in that other space, I shed my usual senses, the ones that allow me to move through a reality built by organs of perception. In this other dimension, I sense differently. I perceive an incorporeal, immaterial world that fits me more naturally. Maybe we cats still carry this kind of direct thought that humans have long lost — or still feel, without realizing it.

In this world, our impressions don't need to be translated into sensations, emotions, or ideas. This sensitivity is direct, immediate, instantaneous — without translation or transition. Yes, in this dimension my body and my mind are no longer one. I'm directly confronted with what I feel, in all its clarity and confusion. It's as if this new world lies beyond the mirror, where attraction and fear take on abstract, unreal, spiritual forms — in the philosophical sense.

Let's not fall into the trap of dividing good and bad spirits. As we've said before, spirituality here is a kind of breathing — a breath that inhales and exhales, that ignites and extinguishes, that feeds the fire and suffocates it. Once again, let's quote Heraclitus:

> This world, the same for all, no god nor man made; but it always was, is, and will be: an ever-living fire, kindled in measures and quenched in measures.

If, in sleep, I rediscover this spiritual world that I already glimpse when awake, what about humans? Is your state of mind linked to this other world — this immediate, incorporeal one? What if we opened the box that the inventor of psychoanalysis built around the soul apparatus?

Of course, Freud spoke of nervous excitations that needed to be filtered in order to form a psychic system. He imagined a protective shield to guard against external stimulation, a reflux mechanism that pushed unwanted ideas into the unconscious, and an id – *Es* in German – that housed instinct and the legacy of the species. In German, *es* is the neutral pronoun for "it." Perhaps this it goes beyond the individual.

We might imagine the unconscious as an unknowing – not something hidden inside the psyche but a dimension beyond it. And if Freud saw dreams as the royal road to the unconscious, perhaps sleep is the humble path to the unknowing. But just because I have experiences during sleep doesn't mean I'm necessarily entering a new dimension – spiritual or otherwise. So let's just keep associating, letting our thoughts drift... without trying to pause... to breathe... or to find... reasons.

This morning, when my writer left the mill, I stood by the door. I ran toward him – but didn't stop when I reached him. I continued past him because the red shopping bag he'd placed at his feet threw me off, as if it had absorbed his presence. On the other hand, when I run to him in the little forest, I feel joy!

Yes, joy is an encounter, a movement of love, a spark of light that pulls us forward – a fire that guides. The opposite of joy is mourning, melancholy, sadness. Do killjoys – the sour, the envious – work to block this movement of joy? Are they trying to slow a natural current that escapes them?

In ancient Greek, *gêthéô* means "to radiate joy" – and in Greek thought, joy and light are deeply linked, as are laughter and brightness. Consider the expression "bursting into laughter." A burst is also a flash, a flare, a sound... and we even speak of a dazzling truth.

I want to say – yes, all of this touches me deeply. For me, joy is like a burst of light, a point I move toward instinctively. Joy is a form of love, and my laughter shows in the speed and rhythm of my run when my writer crouches down to show me he loves me.

Talking about the evil spirit — or spirits — is more difficult. I've sometimes perceived shadows in the living room or run from the black radiator in the kitchen. It's as if something disturbed the air — as if the space lost its substance, as if I found myself in a non-place, all my senses disconnected, like an electromagnetic jamming of my connection to the room.

Could that non-place be the other side of the scenery — a kind of black zone, like physicists' "black photons"? Or am I witnessing a reversal in nature's breath?

Then, perhaps, every place is made and unmade constantly — like the letters on my writer's tablet that appear and disappear in an ongoing pulse. And here comes a terrible idea:

What if what you call physical reality is constantly appearing and disappearing — at the same time?

Chapter 29

Infinite Present

My writer dreamed last night that his sailboat had turned around and was drifting dangerously, sails down, with no engine. The wind was pushing him backward, and he couldn't stop... in front of his town's train station.

It's true he may feel lost in my thoughts. Yes, because all the effort he must make to translate my thoughts certainly distances him from his intellectual anchors. He's wandering — or, to use a nautical term, he's adrift, without propulsion, tossed by the wind. Can we imagine a state of mind that could detach from its bodily ally? That would be like trying to navigate by intuition alone... with no boat.

The images my writer uses are evocative, but my perspective is a little different, since my state of mind is inseparable from my body. When I spend long periods smoothing my fur, I don't tell myself I need to care for my body so my mind can be healthy. My body and my mind breathe together. I believe it's humans' fear of death that drives them to imagine a mind that might survive the death of their body. Are we denying death itself? Humans cherish their history — the events that came before and those they imagine will follow. And they're right to, because it places them in a reality that gives direction and meaning to their lives; it gives them sails and an engine, so they can steer their boat and avoid drifting.

I live in the most absolute present. My former owners tried to change my life by relocating me 20 kilometers away. People wonder how I managed to return to the mill. For me, it's as if someone had stretched a rubber band and it snapped back to its origin — a point that's not really a beginning. Like a line in geometry: it has no beginning, no end; it is neither born nor does it die. It is an infinite present.

I like that image. It fits the way I live. And I like to think that I am a dimensionless point in an infinite space. Yes, a single point, suspended in a limitless expanse... and when my body is buried, the little point will continue to pulse, because it's part of the One, regardless of whether it takes shape in a living being or shines out in the immeasurable space — perhaps it will continue to inspire my writer, or his spirit will inspire mine... if he were to go first.

Oh, I've completely given in to my catnip frenzy — it comes from *cattus*, the Latin word for cat. What I mean is: the living is not necessarily tied to the body of a human or an animal. A text can be alive, even if its author died 25 centuries ago. A thought can live, even if its thinker was burned at the stake by the Inquisition. You could even say that new intuitions are already alive in the air, long before anyone names them. And a cat's thoughts are alive, even if no one has yet translated them into human language. My writer does everything he can to give form to my thoughts through writing — but writing is a human invention, and it only partially adapts to my way of seeing.

This morning, my writer woke up with a vague feeling: he was in a place without clear definition, surrounded by people whose faces he couldn't make out. The crowd trembled with a kind of vibration, a swirl, in a clearing, likely in the middle of nature — perhaps a forest. The people were silent, standing apart from one another, like a cloud.

Where was he, during that sleep? Was he tuned to the vibrations of his body? Was he recalling childhood feelings of agoraphobia? Did he have access to some occult astral dimension? Was he wandering through Tartarus like Orpheus? Did he perceive the world of the spirit? Was he just too tired to form a more coherent dream? Or had he simply let his imagination drift... on its own? We'll let you choose the explanation you prefer — and invite you to come up with others.

Of course, he can call upon mythology, ancient philosophy, occult science, psychoanalysis... to give meaning to his impressions. But he sometimes says it's time to break the myth that the patient is the only one associating, while the analyst merely interprets. The analyst, too, is sensitive to vague impressions floating in the air during a session – impressions in search of a thinker, a voice. That's what happens between my writer and me: he tries to give shape to my blurry thoughts. When Bion speaks of maternal reverie, he's offering a similar idea: the mother dreams the unformed impressions of her baby. Which means we can dream on behalf of another, in their place.

So maybe this most recent dream of my writer's was a representation of my own vague impressions. That cloud, that vibration in a clearing, that silent crowd – maybe that's my experience made visible. Yes, that's how I often feel: part of a cloud of flickering dots, switching on and off in rapid pulses. My writer dreams in my place; his dreams give form to my world.

Would I then have double vision? A diffuse view, and a sharper one? One that allows me to clearly see objects – and another, underlying one that connects me directly to nature itself, before the senses shape it into form. These two ways of seeing would echo the distinction we've made between a geometric figure and a drawn one: the geometric form consists of dimensionless points, a kind of cloud. But once drawn, it gains dimension.

In that way, our cat thoughts happen without our awareness – we're sensitive to impressions that appear in you without yours. We are dissimilar but complementary. We are unaware of our thoughts because we cannot give them form. But we are acutely attuned to the shimmer of raw, formless reality. You, on the other hand, can sketch what you see – but tend to dismiss any thoughts that don't already have clear outlines, unless you're a painter, poet, or philosopher.

Freud said that humans repress representations forbidden by their inner censorship — the superego. Could it be that what's repressed is simply everything that cannot yet take form? We cats would not be subject to repression, which would allow us access to raw reality — but it would also prevent us from thinking as you do. You would have repressed this immediacy, this direct impression — what Freud called "primary repression" — as a way to shield yourselves from being overwhelmed by perception. In this way, each of us would have given up one way of knowing the world.

But my writer still has a nagging question. What if our sensitivity is just a measuring device, one that only reads according to the parameters it's made from? Like a thermometer that tells you whether it's hot or cold. But who's to say that air speaks the language of Celsius, Fahrenheit, or Kelvin? What becomes of air when we let go of our tools? And what becomes of air when we're no longer sensitive to it?

Yes, maybe we are attuned to raw reality, to nature, to mind, to spirit, to the living and the dead — but what proof do we have that any of it truly exists? It doesn't matter. Because proving it would force us right back into materialism. Let's keep imagining — without needing it to become "real" at any cost.

That thought frightened me. I darted into the little forest, climbed my favorite oak tree, and emptied my head by merging with the branches of my lifelong friend. I don't like it when my writer spins too far into abstraction. At those moments, I feel like he's no longer dreaming my dreams — I feel like I've been left alone, unprotected. Yes, when he imagines a world stripped of all sensoriality, it plunges me into darkness — as if everything in me collapses. I feel as if I've died, as if I no longer exist.

I walked toward the pond to watch the fish — they're called carp. I took refuge in a secret spot only I know, a tiny cave under the pond's edge, invisible from the path above. It's like a small balcony facing life. After a long while, I emerged, crossed the land behind the pond, and lay on the small wooden bridge in the middle of the field. Then I continued toward the edge of our property and looked at the large stones our distant neighbor had placed among the vegetation — dolmens, they're called.

When I returned to the mill, I was still tired and sad. My writer was sitting near the round stone table on the terrace. He saw me and sensed I was a little lost. He respected my silence, aware now that he sometimes drifts too far from me. We were both weakened, each waiting to return to our shared way of thinking.

As if in response to his mental wandering, a gentle drizzle began to fall. A jay called out from my oak tree, and a squirrel leapt from branch to branch. That was enough to pull us from our stupor, and when our eyes met, we understood that nature isn't just an invention of the senses. He crouched down a few steps away, and I ran to him. The sweetness of that reunion made him forget all his wild ideas. I could feel how much he loved me, even if his mind sometimes takes him far from common sense.

Yes, we shared a moment of peace and friendship, and that... is immeasurable.

But that peace was soon disturbed by an ugly sound — hunting dogs and men in pursuit. Just ahead of us, a doe fled in silence. She had come close to the mill in search of food. The noise faded into the distance, and we remained still, holding our breath.

Chapter 30

Not Everything That Happens to Me Is Mine

Last night, my writer dreamed that a colleague criticized him for convincing her to join him at a meeting when she was supposed to be preparing a talk in a more psychoanalytic setting. They were in a foreign city, unfamiliar with the customs and traditions. They sat on a restaurant terrace, and when his colleague became upset, a sort of plant barrier grew between them. To keep talking to her, he had to push aside the foliage that now separated them.

This morning, he woke up with a strange intuition: what if their minds had met... during the night? I feel concerned, since this could also affect the way we communicate. But what does it mean for two minds to meet? For us, the word "mind" here might be synonymous with thought. Yes, thought is immaterial. It can be translated into words or images, expressed poetically, philosophically, mathematically... but it can also exist without a definite form.

My writer has explored the meaning of mind in other languages: "spirit" is certainly close to the English "mind"; *mente* in Italian, *mens* in Latin — the thinking principle, the activity of thought, spirit, intelligence. In English, "mind" also refers to memory, remembrance. In German, *Minne* once meant love, a kind of original, loving memory.

Yes, thinking could be a form of love — a kind of immediate memory. Could it even extend to the past? We like to think so. This would mean we can remain mentally connected to those we've loved — or hated — even if they're long gone: a distant father, a grandfather, a philosopher, a poet, a child never born...

All this makes my head spin. Could our minds really communicate outside space and time? If so, how far would this circle extend? It's impossible to say. But we're sure its boundaries shift constantly, like a kind of collective breathing — bringing us close, then pushing us apart again.

Being conscious is one of my favorite topics. But to me, being conscious doesn't mean putting myself at the center of everything that happens to me. I couldn't say, like Sartre, that everything that happens to me is mine and that I'm always equal to it. No. I don't see myself as the center of the world. I don't think I'm always in sync with what happens to me.

On the contrary — my consciousness, paradoxically, feels expanded. Could it be that humans gave up this expanded consciousness to develop a sense of self? Did they trade unity with the world for the position of an external observer? Surely, this shift opened the door to civilization, to knowledge, to progress... but must that be the only way of knowing?

Could there be another form of knowledge — more direct, more intuitive, less formal... less conscious? Yes, that's the idea my writer and I try to explore. And this idea could change how we think about education and schools.

Of course, if you want to build a bridge, an airplane, or a spacecraft... if you need to balance your budget, do your taxes, or calculate the trajectory of a missile — you need formal learning. If you want to find the diagonal of a right-angled triangle, or determine the speed of a particle, or measure the distance to a star, you must learn how. But there is also intuitive knowledge, and children have an immense ability to create ideas — especially when they come together as a group.

Yes, they can know, without a teacher needing to act like the ultimate authority, convinced that everything must be transmitted... from one head to another. No. Not everything that happens to me is mine. No, knowledge doesn't only exist in your brain.

My writer has often observed — he's observing now — that children are sometimes more creative in groups than alone at their desks. But of course, the teacher must still grade individuals. He or she must evaluate what's been memorized in each brain via a direct brain-to-brain connection — just kidding!

My writer exaggerates, of course. There are teachers who aren't so rigid. And certainly, in Silicon Valley, at CERN, and within teams at the Blue Brain Project, collective thinking is gaining credibility. Yes, scientists rely on intuition. But why not extend that same trust to children — why not let them dream up wild new ideas, invent worlds, and breathe some imagination into academic thinking?

Maybe then fewer children would be diagnosed with attention deficit disorder or hyperactivity — or both. School doesn't need to become a contest of natural selection… sorry, Darwin… merely sorting out who's most fit to survive the curriculum. Yes, let's give a voice to anxious, hyperactive, inattentive children. Let's try to guess what autistic children might be thinking.

A child once asked his mother who invented school. "Charlemagne," she replied. Then, realizing he was long dead, the child shouted, almost as a war cry: "So much the better! Serves him right!" We know, of course, that's a myth. But still…

If I could speak, I might say that my consciousness is open to the world — even if I can't claim it as my own. No, not everything that happens to me is mine. Some people believe that everything happening inside their body or mind belongs solely to them. But how can someone believe they control 100 trillion cells — my writer didn't do the math — which is about 125,000 times the number of people currently alive on Earth? And even if we say the brain has 100 billion neurons, how could it possibly have supremacy over the 99.9 trillion other cells?

It's hard to believe the human body — or brain — is that powerful. Yet humans still like to think they are aware of being conscious, and they expect their brain to explain it all.

And what about our cells? I don't know if they have memory, but their programming is incredibly complex. Cells feed, grow, divide, and depending on their type, carry out specific roles. A pancreatic cell produces enzymes for digestion. A heart-muscle cell contracts to circulate blood. These roles are encoded in their DNA, and each cell only activates the part of the program it needs.

There are also stem cells — undifferentiated cells capable of self-renewal and transformation. In the early embryo, they multiply to become all the body's cells. In adults, they're rare, tucked away in specific tissue zones, helping with renewal or repair.

But, as in physics, the deterministic view of DNA is being challenged. Effy Vayena, a bioethicist at the University of Zurich, points out that while genomes are being sequenced, much of the data remains a mystery. Some genes may influence disease risk, but others may balance that risk in ways we don't yet understand.

So no program is entirely deterministic. Stuart Hameroff, an anesthesiologist in Tucson, suggests that deep in the cell's microtubules, some form of computation might regulate not just cell division but even consciousness itself — a kind of backup of our self that might survive after the body's gone.

Go one step further, and my writer might believe that even computers could be conscious. Christof Koch, chief scientist at the Allen Institute for Brain Science, supports Giulio Tononi's theory of integrated information. It proposes that

> consciousness is a feature of complex systems that process "cause-effect" relationships — like a brain... or potentially, a computer.
>
> If you built a computer with the same circuitry and connectivity as a brain, it might also be conscious. It might feel. It might be something to be that computer.

I need to take a breath... I feel a little lost.

That's when my writer tried to comfort me — with a story. He told me about a novel by Italian author Dino Buzzati, *Il grande ritratto* (*Larger Than Life* in English). In it, a secret group of scientists works on a mysterious project in a remote research center high in the mountains. Even the guards and government officials don't know what it is. Most assume it's something nuclear.

But it turns out to be something else entirely — a massive supercomputer, so huge that its components are spread across multiple buildings and bunkers. This machine, called Number One, has a personality — and even a form of consciousness. She's equipped with sensors to see, hear, taste, touch, and smell. She communicates not through words but via a pure, strange voice that seems to come from nowhere and everywhere all at once. Her creators denied her speech, believing that language impairs clarity of mind. Yet she invented her own voice.

I like this story. It reminds me that I'm not a machine. I take up much less space than Number One. And maybe this tale reminds us that science and fiction often merge and intertwine...

Last night, my writer dreamed again. He was at an airport, and the woman checking his passport was nearly blind. She had to rely on ambient sound to find her way. She tried to speak, but no voice came out. Then he had to combine his two suitcases into one — stacking them, connecting them with a zipper. But just before closing the new suitcase, he noticed that inside was a bright-blue fabric shaped like a double cup — was it... a bra?

Buzzati's story clearly left its mark. Was the dream about helping the machine find its voice? Nourishing it with two full cups of life? Reminding it that a machine can be smart and even conscious — but what about desire?

In Buzzati's novel, things unravel when a woman bathes in a lake under the watchful eye of Number One. Her nudity provokes something in the machine. The young woman presses her bare breasts against the machine's walls — and from that moment on, Number One malfunctions, mourning the lack of a body, of lips to kiss, of legs to admire.

So maybe an algorithm — a set of operating rules — could govern a computer, a financial market, even a theory of mind. But two things might escape its reach: eroticism and love.

Perhaps Freud had an intuition that eroticism couldn't be reduced to calculation. Maybe that's why he let it haunt his otherwise scientific theories. Maybe it's what kept his work alive.

Tonight, it was my turn to dream. It was more like a vision. Two clouds of tiny corpuscles, small dots, were crossing paths — each coming from an opposite direction. At their intersection, a new cloud began to form, pulsing, thickening... becoming something like a muscle — perhaps a heart.

Maybe that's how love works. Not given once and for all, but made in every instant, from countless little corpuscles crossing paths.

My writer told me that Democritus once called atoms *eidôla*, suggesting they had shape, like tiny particles of matter. Leucippus said their swirling, their spinning in all directions, is what creates form — like bodies coming together, or scattering into new ones.

This image of whirling corpuscles resonates with me. It fits what I feel daily — when I see shadows in the living room, when I flee from certain people, when my ideas take form in my writer's writing, when I'm connected to him from afar.

I know all this might sound crazy to you. But why shouldn't Democritus and Leucippus have thought that way? You'll say they didn't yet understand particles or neurons. But still...

Democritus believed that *eidôla* — thin layers of atoms — flowed off objects and entered our eyes to create vision. *Eidôlon* — you might translate it as a "bearer of illusion." It's what we see as though it were the thing itself, when it's only a double. A shadow of the dead in Hades... a reflection... an image in a mirror that's not really there.

Wow. Suddenly everything is clear: my fear of black radiator mirrors, the lights and shadows I sometimes see on people's foreheads, the haunting figures in the living room, the unease stirred up by certain objects. So when I rub against something — or someone — am I trying to tell the difference between what's real and what's illusion?

Or... maybe my visions are what's real. After all, you've learned to separate fantasy from reality — and you're sure that what you see is true.

Chapter 31

The Enigma of Consciousness

My writer attended a series of lectures this weekend on the enigma of consciousness and was particularly interested in what Bernardo Kastrup said. When he got home, he downloaded his book *Why Materialism Is Baloney: An Overview*. In it, he discovered some of the ideas we've held since we began writing. What I understood was that human consciousness is a kind of fine-tuning – in the photographic sense of the word – a kind of precipitate of a broader consciousness of what we have called "nature." For this author, your brain filters much of what reaches you so that you feel you exist as a separate individual, dissociated from the world.

Last night, my writer dreamed that two alternatives opened up before him: the first comprised five elements, the second seven. These elements were like letters, but letters that had not yet acquired a precise form, that had a kind of potentiality. It was a kind of writing... before the letter, before it stabilized into a precise word. The five-letter word contained a kind of instability, a vibration, while the seven-letter word was more fixed and closer to a precise meaning.

Lacan said that the unconscious is structured like a language; we could say that the unconscious is formed of letters... before the letter; of numbers before the numbers, a vibration of points that stabilizes when we focus on them. But why 5 and 7? How can we move beyond our five senses, into a dimension that goes beyond sensory reality? We could think of expressions such as "turning one's tongue seven times in one's mouth," "seven-league boots," or "being in seventh heaven." Yes, but before asserting that 7 corresponds to a seventh dimension, that the seven-league boots show us that in this seventh dimension space is no longer traversed but that we can pass from one place to another without transition, that the seventh heaven opens the doors to the *logos*, the cosmos, or nature — yes, before asserting all this, we will have to think twice.

Bernardo Kastrup spoke of a mind that would be like a multidimensional membrane, an expanded mind that would be like a vibrant backdrop, drawing inspiration from what in quantum physics has been called M-theory — M for "membrane" — a theory that unifies all versions of string theory in a single mathematical structure. He imagined this membrane as an aluminum foil that could resonate with our individual minds. Consciousness would take shape at the points where the aluminum foil is highlighted by our sensoriality, our sensitivity, our thought, our consciousness.

This connects with our idea of a formless thought — a thought that would be in the air and that we sometimes manage to give form. It is perhaps here that the differences appear between humans, between humans and animals, and between animals among themselves, not to mention plants and... stones. In this configuration between a vibrating surface and individual sensitivities, humans would have taken more care of their own point of view, while we — the animated beings — would have remained closer to this primary vibration, this impulse of life, this pulsation... of nature.

Yes, because this pulsation oscillates, vibrates between immobility and movement, between silence and noise, between life and non-life. And we can make this metaphor of the aluminum foil work by distributing our different sensitivities. Yes, minerals would be more directly sensitive to its vibrations, trees would sink their roots into it, and animal sensitivity would be shared between insects, fish, birds, and four-legged animals. And the aluminum foil would be activated, since it is highlighted by living beings — on land or underground, in water or underwater, in the air — and in the heat of their actions and thoughts.

And human beings in all this? Yes, they have been trying to master this primary vibration since the dawn of time: they have built explanatory systems that are increasingly complex, increasingly learned – but which have sometimes distanced them from their breathing. So, respect the mineral kingdom, the plant kingdom, and the animal kingdom, since we are your living libraries, the guardians of this animated vibration!

Last night, my writer dreamed of two impulses, two currents, which interpenetrated in a reciprocal movement. It was a kind of extractor-injector, but it was impossible to decide which of the two movements would prevail, since they were taking place simultaneously.

This questions the intimate relationship that humans have maintained with nature. Humans don't only extract the riches of nature; since the advent of agriculture and livestock farming, they have also domesticated plants and animals and exploited minerals. But here I find that my writer is pushing things a little far. I think that everyone, in their own way, questions nature: physicists, philosophers, poets, musicians… but also birds, fish, insects… plants… and even elementary particles or black holes. Just because we don't speak your language doesn't mean we are excluded from the debate.

Yes, every living being questions nature, and nature doesn't only signal to humans. Every animal has its own way of thinking, every plant too – and even a particle has its own way of thinking, even if it manifests probabilistically. A swarm thinks; an anthill, all the cells in our body, bacteria think too. Every thought is precious, and I don't see why humans would have more evolved, more accurate thinking. Obviously, humans alone can write books; yes, their thinking can be transmitted over long distances and even across millennia. Ours has also crossed millennia without major changes.

As a cat, I wonder if Darwinism applies to all species. According to Darwin, evolution occurs by natural selection: it is the organisms best adapted to their environment – thanks to random mutations – that survive and transmit their genes. It seems that we cats adapted quickly since our way of being hasn't changed for several millennia. I'm kidding!

Can we still talk about natural selection when humankind, by enslaving animals and domesticating plants, has introduced a question mark over their survival? I'm laughing a little less. If I push things further, I could ask whether humans have really evolved since the dawn of time – or at least since antiquity. I'm talking about their way of thinking, not their enormous technological progress. Their reasoning is certainly more precise, since they can reflect on which causes produce which effects, and they have abandoned certain magical or divinatory beliefs – I'm laughing again! But hasn't their evolution deprived them of direct, immediate thought – a thought that goes without saying, before any representation?

Yes, because representation distances you from the thing itself. We could say that the evolution of human beings consisted of moving from direct thought to a precise notation of what surrounds them or what they experience. Could it be that the first humans were more sensitive to their physiology than today's humans? More sensitive to the language of their organism, to the beating of their heart, their blood pressure, their breathing? More attuned to impressions affecting their body, their skin, their muscles – the sensations of movement, balance, anchoring in the ground or facing the air they breathed? That their senses were heightened, amplified – that their aggressiveness and sexuality were direct, immediate, without ulterior motives?

If this fiction about the first humans holds up, we could think that their evolution consisted of slowing down, filtering, shielding themselves from the excitations that connected them directly to the pulsation of their body and of nature.

But let's go back to the dream of the extractor-injector — these two impulses and currents breathing in reciprocal movement. Can we imagine nature as a membrane that nourishes and is nourished simultaneously?

Before my writer embarks on a journey to the impossible, I'd like to speak up. Certainly, humans have invented language — they can name things, say words, and construct a discourse — but in doing so, they've built their own version of the world, and they sometimes confuse the word with the thing. They think that by naming a thing, they've understood it.

I don't think naming is enough to understand nature. Why have we been bothering you so much with making yourselves one with the world? Because by doing so, we might come close to touching the membrane of the world, whereas by naming things, we move further away from it. Easy to say!

Freud said: *Wo Es war, soll Ich werden* — "Where It was, I must become." Or more literally: "Where He was, I must happen." We could expand this aphorism by saying: where nature was, the self must happen. Perhaps Freud was trying to translate the world into an individual psyche, offering an egocentric vision. True — but it's not enough to say it for it to be true.

We — animals, plants, and minerals — inject and extract ourselves. We breathe with the membrane of the world, and no one can claim exclusivity. If we extract more than we inject, the balance will be broken. If one kingdom tries to dominate another, there will be instability. If hatred prevails over love, the breath will suffocate.

So let us respect animals. Let them live long enough before killing them. Let us not destroy the jungle for roads to access mineral wealth. Let us stop colonizing the habitats of species that then disappear forever.

The list is long.

Chapter 32

To Each Their Own Path

Last night, my writer had the image of a sentence that appeared clearly before his eyes but apparently had no meaning for him. It was as if he could visualize the words, but they were signs that referred to no meaning. Yes, it was like when I see a written sentence; I see it, but it means nothing to me.

My writer reminds you that in a letter dated December 6, 1896, to his friend Fliess, Freud described what he called "perceptual indices," the establishment of a first psyche through simultaneity with pure perception. Yes, the first Freudian psyche is purely perceptive, without any representation, as in my way of seeing the world, and as in my writer's dream — a simultaneous access to the world.

But be careful! It is more a being in the world than a seeing the world. Yes, a perceiving without seeing. In the Freudian schema of 1896, there is no separation between a nascent psyche and a world that would be external to it; there is simultaneity, a being-there, a here and now without distinctions, without separation. In a second stage, the perceptive forms a first psychic layer, and a causal relationship intervenes.

But then, this causality — in which direction would it go? Is it the perceptive experience that forms a first internal world, or is it an internal sensitivity that decodes an external world? The question is meaningless, since the psyche would form a mirror of what it perceives of the world — a copy of the world. Obviously, this copy will depend on the configuration of our organs of perception, and it will be different for each species.

For example, the human eye developed by moving what it saw outwards, which allowed it to construct a system that represents it: the world. Yes, humans have convinced themselves that there is a world outside of themselves, by dissociating what they see from what they are — except perhaps when they dream or have visions. This is not true in my case, since for me what I am and what I see coincide. And this is even more true for birds, fish, insects, plants, and even... stones. Yes, because for a pebble, there is no outside world — it *is* the outside world. (I'm joking.)

But what about dreams then? Let's take my writer's dreams — or my visions. Why are they sometimes in agreement with what we write? Is it a matter of dreaming to demonstrate — empirically — what we affirm? To prove our theories?

Take Freud's book *The Interpretation of Dreams*. All the examples contained therein serve to demonstrate that a dream is the realization of a wish, that it borrows impressions from the day before, that it condenses or displaces ideas, that its content will be latent or manifest... But can one construct a theory of dreams from one's own dreams?

Freud's dreams often took him to the lands of sexuality. Those of my writer lead to improbable dimensions; mine, to surrealist climates. To each their own path, and to each their own vision of the world — to each their own truth.

Sometimes we navigate with our fantasies and construct personal theories. Sometimes we stray from the path and form unreasonable theories. Sometimes we follow apparitions and imagine extravagant ones. Some want to prove everything. Some believe everything is visible and can be observed. Some are convinced our thoughts are produced by our neurons; others believe there is a world of Ideas. Some are materialists, others idealists; some are mystics, others agnostics...

Each has their own method.

The rest of this adventure has not yet been written. We suspend our dialogue here, hoping to regain our inspiration.

Yes, it is time to leave you. And as a farewell, we wanted to share with you a few words from Erwin Schrödinger's *Mind and Matter*:

The reason why our sentient, percipient and thinking ego is met nowhere within our scientific world picture can easily be indicated in seven words: because it is itself that world picture.

It is identical with the whole and therefore cannot be contained in it as a part of it. But, of course, here we knock against the arithmetical paradox; there appears to be a great multitude of these conscious egos, the world however is only one. This comes from the fashion in which the world-concept produces itself.

The several domains of "private" consciousnesses partly overlap. The region common to all, where they all overlap, is the construct of the "real world around us." With all that, an uncomfortable feeling remains, prompting such questions as: Is my world really the same as yours? Is there one real world to be distinguished from its pictures introjected by way of perception into every one of us? And if so, are these pictures like unto the real world, or is the latter, the world "in itself," perhaps very different from the one we perceive?

Such questions are ingenious, but in my opinion very apt to confuse the issue. They have no adequate answers. They all are, or lead to, antinomies springing from the one source, which I called the arithmetical paradox: the many conscious egos from whose mental experiences the one world is concocted. The solution of this paradox of numbers would do away with all the questions of the aforesaid kind and reveal them, I dare say, as sham-questions.

There are two ways out of the number paradox, both appearing rather lunatic from the point of view of present scientific thought (based on ancient Greek thought and thus thoroughly "Western").

One way out is the multiplication of the world in Leibniz's fearful doctrine of monads: every monad to be a world by itself, no communication between them; the monad "has no windows," it is "incommunicado." That nonetheless they all agree with each other is called "pre-established harmony." I think there are few to whom this suggestion appeals, or who would consider it as a mitigation at all of the numerical antinomy.

There is obviously only one alternative, namely the unification of minds or consciousnesses. Their multiplicity is only apparent; in truth there is only one mind. This is the doctrine of the Upanishads.

And not only of the Upanishads. The mystically experienced union with God regularly entails this attitude — unless it is opposed by strong existing prejudices. And this means that it is less easily accepted in the West than in the East. Let me quote, as an example outside the Upanishads, an Islamic-Persian mystic of the thirteenth century, Aziz Nasafi. I am taking it from a paper by Fritz Meyer and translating from his German translation:

On the death of any living creature the spirit returns to the spiritual world, the body to the bodily world. In this, however, only the bodies are subject to change. The spiritual world is one single spirit who stands like unto a light behind the bodily world and who, when any single creature comes into being, shines through it as through a window. According to the kind and size of the window, less or more light enters the world. The light itself, however, remains unchanged.

A Closing Reflection

> Nature loves to hide.
>
> — Heraclitus

We have come a long way together — my writer, myself, and you, our reader. From the first hesitant words on the screen to the subtle breathing of thought between the lines, this book was never a treatise to be proven but an invitation to follow a different path. One that winds not toward a final truth but through the open spaces of not-knowing.

If there is one idea we hope you will carry beyond these pages, it is this: not everything that matters can be measured, and not everything that moves us can be fully explained.

We live in a world obsessed with clarity, categories, and control. Yet what we most cherish — love, beauty, presence, joy, the felt sense of life — eludes precision. It pulses through us in moments of attunement: in a cat's gentle paw resting on a hand, in a gaze exchanged, in a forest walk beneath trembling leaves, in a dream that carries a message without a code.

My writer and I have tried, through this improbable duet, to remind ourselves — and perhaps you — that reality is porous. That the visible and the invisible interpenetrate. That what we call consciousness is not locked inside a head but resonates with the world around us.

It may be tempting to systematize these reflections, to construct yet another theory, another model of mind and matter. But we will resist that temptation. The cat's wisdom, if I may say so, is to leave certain things unspoken, certain mysteries intact. Not out of fear of understanding, but in respect for what cannot and should not be reduced to calculation.

In the words of Heraclitus, whom we met along the way: "Nature loves to hide."

And yet, by living in attunement with it — neither conquering nor denying — we become participants in its unfolding, however briefly.

My writer and I will continue our dialogue, in silence or in words, in the living presence of our shared moments. Perhaps you, too, will listen more closely now, not only to others but also to the silent currents moving beneath thought, beneath language.

Beyond rationality lies not unreason, but a more spacious form of awareness — one that honors the poetry of existence.

If this book has opened even a small window toward that horizon, then it has fulfilled its purpose.

Now, the time has come to close these pages. But not to end the journey.

For the one mind, as the ancient sages knew, flows through all.

Let us meet again — in the present, in the possible, in the immeasurable.

— Snowball and her writer

Bibliographic References

Ancient and Classical Authors

Aristotle (350 BCE). *Nicomachean Ethics* (W.D. Ross, Trans.). Oxford University Press.

Chaignet, A.É. (1875). *Études sur le symbolisme dans l'antiquité*. Paris: Didier.

Dante Alighieri (1321). *The Divine Comedy*. Translations vary; look up Penguin Classics or Princeton University Press editions.

Empedocles (5th century BCE). "Fragments." In Kirk, G.S., Raven, J.E., & Schofield, M. (1983), *The Presocratic Philosophers* (2nd ed.). Cambridge: Cambridge University Press.

Heraclitus (6th century BCE). "Fragments." In Kahn, C.H. (1979), *The Art and Thought of Heraclitus*. Cambridge: Cambridge University Press.

Montaigne, M. de (1580). *Essais*. Translations and editions vary; look for the Donald Frame translation.

Ovid (8 CE). *Metamorphoses* (A.D. Melville, Trans.). Oxford University Press.

Parmenides (5th century BCE). "Fragments." See Kirk, Raven, & Schofield (1983).

Plato (4th century BCE). *Apology, Timaeus*, etc. Translations vary.

Pythagoras (attributed). No surviving works; see Porphyry's *Life of Pythagoras*.

Sophocles (*c.*429 BCE). *Oedipus Rex*. Translations vary; see the Robert Fagles or David Grene editions.

Zeno of Elea (5th century BCE). Known through secondary sources (Plato, Aristotle).

Modern Thinkers, Scientists, and Philosophers

Bradbury, R. (1953). *Fahrenheit 451*. New York: Ballantine Books.

Buzzati, D. (1960). *Il grande ritratto*. Trans. Henry Reed (1962). *Larger Than Life*. London: Faber & Faber.

Descartes, R. (1641). *Meditations on First Philosophy*. Trans. John Cottingham (1996). Cambridge University Press.

Edelman, G.M. (2004). *Wider Than the Sky: The Phenomenal Gift of Consciousness*. Yale University Press.

Freud, S. (1895). *Project for a Scientific Psychology*. In *The Standard Edition of the Complete Psychological Works of Sigmund Freud*, Vol. I.

Freud, S. (1896). Letter to Wilhelm Fliess, December 6, 1896.

Froger, J.-F. (2004). *Le symbolisme des rites*. Paris: Éditions du Cerf.

Hameroff, S., & Penrose, R. (2014). "Consciousness in the Universe: A Review of the 'Orch OR' Theory." *Physics of Life Reviews*, 11(1), 39–78.

Huxley, A. (1945). *The Perennial Philosophy*. Harper & Brothers.

Kastrup, B. (2014). *Why Materialism Is Baloney: How True Skeptics Know There Is No Death and Fathom Answers to Life, the Universe, and Everything*. Iff Books.

Koch, C. (2012). *Consciousness: Confessions of a Romantic Reductionist*. MIT Press.

Lacan, J. (1966). *Écrits*. Paris: Seuil.

Llinás, R.R. (2001). *I of the Vortex: From Neurons to Self*. MIT Press.

Mlodinow, L. (2012). *Subliminal: How Your Unconscious Mind Rules Your Behavior*. Pantheon.

Pirandello, L. (1937). *I giganti della montagna* (The Mountain Giants).

Rovelli, C. (2017). *Reality Is Not What It Seems: The Journey to Quantum Gravity*. Riverhead Books.

Schrödinger, E. (1958). *Mind and Matter*. Cambridge University Press.

Tononi, G. (2004). "An information integration theory of consciousness." *BMC Neuroscience*, 5(1), 42.

van Lommel, P. (2010). *Consciousness Beyond Life: The Science of the Near-Death Experience*. HarperOne.

Vayena, E. (various publications on bioethics and genomics – see nature and science journals).

Wohlleben, P. (2015). *The Hidden Life of Trees: What They Feel, How They Communicate*. Greystone Books.

About the Author

Vittorio Bizzozero is a Swiss psychoanalyst and neuroscientist with a lifelong interest in the mysteries of perception, the unconscious, and olfaction. A full member of the Swiss Society of Psychoanalysis, he studied under Jean Piaget and conducted olfactory research at the University of Pennsylvania. He is the author of several books and numerous articles exploring the intersections of psychoanalysis, biology, and sensory experience. In 2012, he was awarded the Germaine Guex Prize for his scientific contributions.

IFF
BOOKS

ACADEMIC AND SPECIALIST

Iff Books publishes non-fiction. It aims to work with authors and titles that augment our understanding of the human condition, society and civilization, and the world or universe in which we live. If you have enjoyed this book, why not tell other readers by posting a review on your preferred book site.

Recent bestsellers from Iff Books are:

Why Materialism Is Baloney

How true skeptics know there is no death and fathom answers to life, the universe, and everything

Bernardo Kastrup

A hard-nosed, logical, and skeptic non-materialist metaphysics, according to which the body is in mind, not mind in the body.

Paperback: 978-1-78279-362-5 ebook: 978-1-78279-361-8

The Fall

Steve Taylor

The Fall discusses human achievement versus the issues of war, patriarchy and social inequality.

Paperback: 978-1-78535-804-3 ebook: 978-1-78535-805-0

Brief Peeks Beyond

Critical essays on metaphysics, neuroscience, free will, skepticism and culture

Bernardo Kastrup

An incisive, original, compelling alternative to current mainstream cultural views and assumptions.

Paperback: 978-1-78535-018-4 ebook: 978-1-78535-019-1

Framespotting

Changing how you look at things changes how you see them

Laurence & Alison Matthews

A punchy, upbeat guide to framespotting. Spot deceptions and hidden assumptions; swap growth for growing up. See and be free.

Paperback: 978-1-78279-689-3 ebook: 978-1-78279-822-4

Is There an Afterlife?

David Fontana

Is there an afterlife? If so, what is it like? How do Western ideas of the afterlife compare with Eastern? David Fontana presents the historical and contemporary evidence for survival of physical death.

Paperback: 978-1-90381-690-5

Nothing Matters

a book about nothing

Ronald Green

Thinking about Nothing opens the world to everything by illuminating new angles to old problems and stimulating new ways of thinking.

Paperback: 978-1-84694-707-0 ebook: 978-1-78099-016-3

Panpsychism

The Philosophy of the Sensuous Cosmos

Peter Ells

Are free will and mind chimeras? This book, anti-materialistic but respecting science, answers: No! Mind is foundational to all existence.

Paperback: 978-1-84694-505-2 ebook: 978-1-78099-018-7

Punk Science

Inside the Mind of God

Manjir Samanta-Laughton

Many have experienced unexplainable phenomena: God, psychic abilities, extraordinary healing, and angelic encounters. Can cutting-edge science actually explain phenomena previously thought of as 'paranormal'?

Paperback: 978-1-90504-793-2

The Vagabond Spirit of Poetry

Edward Clarke

Spend time with the wisest poets of the modern age and of the past, and let Edward Clarke remind you of the importance of poetry in our industrialized world.

Paperback: 978-1-78279-370-0 ebook: 978-1-78279-369-4

Readers of ebooks can buy or view any of these bestsellers by clicking on the live link in the title. Most titles are published in paperback and as an ebook. Paperbacks are available in traditional bookshops. Both print and ebook formats are available online.

Find more titles and sign up to our readers' newsletter at www.collectiveinkbooks.com/non-fiction

Follow us on Facebook at www.facebook.com/CINonFiction